TIARA

• ● •

TIARA

• • •

DIANA SCARISBRICK

CHRONICLE BOOKS

SAN FRANCISCO

IN ASSOCIATION WITH THE MUSEUM OF FINE ARTS, BOSTON

Library of Congress
Cataloging-in-Publication Data available.
ISBN 0-8118-2717-8
Printed in Hong Kong.

Designed by Flux, sf

Distributed in Canada
by Raincoast Books
8680 Cambie Street
Vancouver, British Columbia V6P 6M9

10 9 8 7 6 5 4 3 2 1

Chronicle Books
85 Second Street
San Francisco, California 94105

www.chroniclebooks.com

CONTENTS

Tiaras, by enhancing the dignity and beauty of women, have contributed to the brilliance of so many great events over the past two hundred years, though their history reaches far back into antiquity. Offered as signs of respect from the living to the dead, they crowned the heads of royal and noble mummies in the tombs of the twentieth and twenty-first dynasties (1200–945 B.C.) of ancient Egypt. Some of the most beautiful tiaras were created by the goldsmiths of classical Greece to adorn the statues of divinities and the heads of the priests and sacrificial victims as they processed to the altars of the sanctuaries. These golden ears of wheat, sacred to Demeter, goddess of prosperity, and the intertwined branches of the olive of Athena, the oak of Zeus, the myrtle of Aphrodite, the ivy of Dionysus, and the laurel of Apollo, were celebrated by the poet Sappho (612 B.C.) in an ode (*Athenae XV* 674e). Because of their sacred associations, tiaras were regarded as symbols of honor, awarded to the victors of musical and athletic contests and worn by people of high rank at weddings and banquets. Other Greek tiaras were inspired by flowers, particularly the lily, the honeysuckle, and the rose.

To further the illusion of naturalism, the flowers were mounted on trembler springs, and there might be a bee sucking pollen or a cicada perched on petals. An outstanding garland of this type was found in a tomb at Canosa in southern Italy (third century B.C.): wrought in filigree, the garnet and carnelian flowers, naturalistically enameled in tones that contrast with the luster of the gold ground, are tied with ribbons (Museo Nazionale, Taranto, Italy).

Cecil Beaton photograph of Loelia,
third wife of the second duke
of Westminster (1931), wearing
a *kokoshnik* halo-shaped tiara.

SOTHEBY'S

Besides these garlands and wreaths, there were also gold bands or fillets, stamped with spiral scrolls, lotus flowers, acanthus, palmettes, rosettes, figures—the Muses or divinities—and Gorgon heads to intimidate enemies. Some rise to a pediment in the center, other meet in a Hercules knot, alluding to the unfastening of the bridal garment by the bridegroom and the transition from the unmarried to the married state.

After the Romans adopted the tiara as the supreme indication of rank and honor, it became inseparable from the image of imperial authority. Rich and well-born men and women also wore tiaras, and significantly, when the twenty-year-old Creperia Tryphaena died in A.D. 170, she was buried with her wooden doll and adorned with her jewelry, including a golden myrtle wreath, as a token of her status as an aristocrat. It was the same throughout the Roman Empire, where women of rank were portrayed in painting and sculpture wearing their golden bandeaux low on the forehead or with the wreaths and halos on their heads, which would have shimmered in the sunlight as they moved.

With the emergence of feudalism, head ornaments assumed great importance in medieval society, and pinnacled coronets and circlets of roses, ivy, oak, strawberry leaves, and fleurs-de-lis were part of the attire of kings and queens, lords and ladies. Every well-born woman would expect to receive a "coronal," or jeweled garland, as part of her dowry, to be worn at her wedding: Boccaccio, in the *Decameron* (1349–51), tells how the Marquis of Saluzzo, before his marriage, took time to buy "girdles and rings and a rich and beautiful coronal and all the other things needful to a newly wedded wife." The marriage contract might stipulate the value of the gold, silver, gems, and pearls employed in the execution of the all-important coronal or garland, whose significance was explained by the anonymous English author of *Dives et Pauper* (1405–10): "It betokeneth the gladness and dignitie of wedlocke." However, in the sixteenth century, coronals were displaced by the bilament, the attire, and the aigrette. Head ornaments echoing those of antiquity disappeared until the late eighteenth century, when they returned with the revival of classical principles in art. By this time the character of jewelry had changed, for it was no longer the concern of the goldsmith, but of the stone setter, and the role of gold and silver had been reduced to providing a framework into which diamonds and colored stones could be set to create the maximum *éclat*. In England the tiaras worn by Queen Charlotte, wife of George III, were mounted with the splendid diamonds given to her by the Indian princes subject to British rule. Two were floral diamond bandeaux, one hung with emerald drops, the other combined with colored gems. A third, "a most magnificent bandeau of uncommon splendor and immense value composed of large collets of nine brilliants of matchless size and perfection," was admired at the reception she held in honor of the king's birthday on June 4, 1799. Her example was followed by the aristocracy. A diamond tiara centered on a heart motif flanked by running scrolls and interspersed with trumpet- and star-shaped flowers was made for Viscountess Montagu in 1767: her descendant, Lady Diana Spencer, wore it over her wedding veil when

Bust of the Roman Lady Aththaia
(A.D. 150–200) wearing a veil,
jewels in her hair, and a bandeau
across her forehead.

she married the Prince of Wales in 1981. A floral tiara set with 235 brilliant-cut diamonds made by the French jeweler John Duval for the Baroness de Grey of Wrest Park, Bedfordshire, was only one of many such commissions, for it was now that the tiara came to assume the preeminent role among the jeweled ornaments of English women of rank and wealth, a role it has retained ever since. Whereas in other countries the sight of a tiara might arouse animosity, to the British public it was—for a long time—a source of pride, reflecting national prosperity and greatness.

A foreign traveler observed in the *Lady's Magazine* (1807) that "envy which appears to disunite men in other countries is a vice rare in England." He concluded that the ostentatious display of marks of privilege was accepted in England because the flourishing state of agriculture, trade, and industry was due to the efforts of so many men of high birth. Then the English custom of elevating to the aristocracy men such as Admiral Nelson, who had rendered important services to the country, was much to its advantage. This process continued throughout the nineteenth century, when those who made huge fortunes through industry and business were able to join the ranks of aristocracy, which thus became what the architectural historian J. Mordaunt Crook, in *The Rise of the Nouveaux Riches* (1999), called "a self-renewing plutocracy."

Made for the Viscountess Montagu in 1767, this tiara features continuous running scrolls meeting to form a heart-shaped motif in the center, a design that was revived for the garland style in the early twentieth century. It is a Spencer family heirloom and was worn by Lady Diana Spencer at her wedding to the Prince of Wales in 1981.

EARL SPENCER

In France the tiara was used by Napoleon as a means of asserting the authority of absolute power. His precedent was imperial Rome, and just as Augustus, his empress, and their successors wore tiaras as symbols of their sovereignty, so did Napoleon and the women of his court. His first wife, Josephine, had already adopted the neoclassical tiara during the Consulate, appearing at a reception fashionably "clad in pale pink net scintillating with gold and silver stars, her hair wreathed with diamond ears of corn." She is crowned as empress with a diamond laurel wreath on her head in J. L. David's painting of the coronation of 1804, and each of her sisters-in-law is also wearing a tiara, masterpieces of the court jewelers Nitot & Fils, Marguerite, Foncier, and Sensier. More than any other jewel it was the glittering head ornaments that transformed the women of the parvenue Bonaparte family into royalty. Since the intention was to link them with the glories of ancient Rome, all the designs are strictly classical; that is, symmetrical, simple and clear, with the decorative motifs—pediments, lyres, honeysuckle, laurel palmettes, spiral scrolls, and Greek-key patterns—derived from antiquity. In the same spirit are Empire tiaras mounted with cameos and intaglios carved from hard stones, shell, or coral, illustrating scenes from classical history and mythology or portraits of divinities and heroes. Much to the annoyance of the curators, eighty-six cameos and intaglios were removed from the former royal collection in the Cabinet des Médailles for a *parure*, or a matched set of ornaments, including a tiara, for Empress Josephine. Then, after the divorce of 1809, they were not returned, but reset into a new parure for her successor, Empress Marie Louise. The quantity of pearls and diamonds used to frame these gems is proof of the huge value placed on them, whether they were ancient, or bought from the contemporary artists then working in Rome and Naples. Less expensive versions, with enameled gold leaves converging on a single cameo mounted as a medallion in the center, were available for those who wanted to follow fashion but could not afford costly settings.

Even more splendid than the jewels of the Empress Josephine were those created for the Habsburg Archduchess Marie Louise, who became Napoleon's second wife in 1810. Whether for official use or for her private collection, each parure of matching ornaments included a tiara, crown, and comb, emphasizing the head and proclaiming her rank as a consort of the most powerful man of his time. The grandest, an all-white parure of diamonds, is depicted in a portrait of the empress by Robert Lefèvre: for Bernard Morel, author of *The French Crown Jewels* (1988), this parure "was the most fabulous of the whole of the 19th century."

Since it was Napoleon's wish that his court should be the most brilliant in Europe and thus reflect his imperial grandeur, all the women invited to the ceremonies at his palaces were expected to wear the picturesque court dress, and jewels on their heads and at the neck, wrists, and ears. The effect was evoked by Balzac in *La Paix du Ménage:* "Diamonds glittered everywhere—so much so that it seemed that the entire wealth of the world was concentrated in the salons of Paris . . . never had the diamond been so sought after, never had it been cut and set so as to resemble a display of fireworks."

These diamonds could be seen at their best in the tiara, for as John Mawe observed in his *Treatise on Diamonds and Precious Stones* (1823), while other gems, inserted into rings and bracelets, are enjoyed by the wearer herself and almost entirely lost on the distant beholder, the diamond "blazing on the crown of state, in courts and feasts and high solemnities wreathing itself with the hair . . . proclaims to the surrounding crowd the person of the monarch, of the knight, and of the beauty." He explained that this was due to the diamond's property of absorbing "the pure solar ray and then reflecting it with undiminished intensity and unyielding brilliancy." This was well understood by those who wore tiaras, and diamonds were always mounted in the grandest designs.

French fashion plate (1805) showing court dress and laurel tiara.

MUSEUM OF FINE ARTS, BOSTON

The custom of mourning was scrupulously observed in all European countries during the nineteenth century. In the Empire period, Empress Josephine owned at least one parure of jet, consisting of a bandeau and comb for the head, earrings, necklace, and bracelets, which were listed in the inventory drawn up after her death in 1813. Similarly, Empress Marie Louise bought a full set of mourning jewelry or *parure de grand deuil* from the jewelers Friese & Devillers in 1811. Arriving in London on Christmas Eve in 1817, immediately after the death of Princess Charlotte of Wales in childbirth, American envoy Richard Rush was struck by the solemn effect created by the national expression of bereavement. There were strict regulations prescribing the right attire and accessories. *The Mirror of Fashion* (1821) recommended as "mourning grand costume" after the death of George III a "petticoat robe of black crape over a white slip of gros de Naples, the petticoat trimmed at the border with white crape in festoons. The body of black satin, richly ornamented with black crape, and a train of black satin. Tiara diadem of jet. Black chamois shoes and black gloves. Negligée necklace and earrings of jet." Similar jet ornaments were stipulated by the Earl Marshal so that ladies might "testify to the regret most feel" on the death of George IV (1830). Jet, which could be faceted and polished to gleam attractively, was a court favorite. Upon the death in 1849 of Queen Victoria's mother, the duchess of Kent, Princess Mary of Cambridge put on her jet tiara with her black crape and told a friend how splendid she looked in it. Black ostrich feathers usually completed this attire, adding to the somber effect. Queen Victoria's determination to wear her widow's weeds permanently after the death of Prince Albert in 1861 set the pattern for English women until her own death in 1901. At her funeral "the Royal Princesses all in deep mourning with crape veils and the broad white ribbon of the Victorian order across their breasts looked like abbesses belonging to some religious order," according to Lady Battersea. It was the same elsewhere in Europe, not only as a mark of respect when royalty died but as a demonstration of private grief at the loss of family and friends. Since the

Cut-steel tiara (c.1860), English or French.

MUSEUM OF FINE ARTS, BOSTON

Plate 17. Vol. 2.

This print, published in *Ackermann's Repository of the Arts* (1809), is of a disconsolate widow wearing mourning jewelry with her weeds and her small daughter also in black.

custom was so prevalent and the periods of mourning frequent and lengthy, there was always a demand for the ornaments suitable to wear with the black clothes of full mourning and the gray and lilac of half mourning. For the head, the most common tiaras were made of jet, Berlin iron, cut steel, and black enamel, and they were often worn en suite with necklace, earrings, and bracelet.

ROMANTICISM

Because he was a patron of the art of jewelry, Napoleon had a long lasting influence. First, he reinstated Paris as the creative center—lost during the years of anarchy following the revolution of 1789—so successfully that the city maintained the lead right up to the outbreak of World War II. Second, he demonstrated that jewelry was a most effective means of affirming political prestige and authority. This lesson was not lost on the restored Bourbon monarchs, Louis XVIII and Charles X, who ruled from 1815 to 1830. They, too, encouraged the Parisian jewelers by holding exhibitions at the Louvre, and by having the state collection, so enriched by Napoleon, remodeled for their niece, the Duchesse d'Angoulême, to display at court. Even though Louis Philippe, who became king of France in 1830, did not want the crown jewels on show, his wife, Marie Amélie, born a Bourbon princess, had fine jewels of her own and acquired more from Bapst, the court jewelers; J.B. Fossin, predecessor of Chaumet; and Mellerio. Her receptions at the Tuileries were considered splendid, as *Les Lettres Parisiennes* (1836) described: "Three rows of bejeweled women were paraded before the queen. On every side, the eyes were dazzled by the radiance of the colors darting out from the emeralds and rubies. The sight of those serried ranks of women crowned with so many precious stones had the same effect as an illumination made of colored glass." The tiaras attracted attention not only at court but also at the balls held in embassies and at the private mansions of the rich financial and banking class of the Chaussée d'Antin.

Louis Hersent portrait of Queen Marie Amélie (c.1840) wearing her diamond and sapphire jewelry with pearl, diamond, and sapphire tiara in front of her velvet toque with plumes nodding behind. The necklace, which was bought from Queen Hortense, dates from the Empire period.

MUSÉE CONDÉ, CHANTILLY

This was a time when the best tiaras were worn by English women. The tiara of the duchess of Sutherland, seen at one of the grand balls held by Louis Philippe and Marie Amélie at the Tuileries, was valued at 8,000 pounds, and another, belonging to the marchioness of Conygnham, was almost as splendid. These tiaras reflected the mood of euphoria that followed the victory over Napoleon at Waterloo, which coincided with the huge rise in rents for agricultural, town, and industrial property. Thus enriched, the aristocracy indulged in purchases of great silver services for display at the table and suites of jewelry for the women. These suites almost always included a tiara, and at the coronation of George IV in Westminster Abbey, according to the *Lady's Magazine* (1821), "coronets, tiaras, circlets, aigrettes, combs of diamonds, pearls and colored gems were mingled with the feathers of the headdress . . . among the colored gems the pink topaz was the most prevalent . . . pearl bandeaux brought low across the forehead were very general. The feathers were of the most superb description and the plumes very full . . . they were mostly placed far back." These plumes, believed to recall the victory of the Black Prince and Edward III over the

Alexandre François Caminade portrait of the Duchesse d'Angoulême (c.1820) in court dress with plumes and long, lace-trimmed train, wearing a parure that includes her diamond tiara.

CHATEAU DE VERSAILLES

Diamond and emerald tiara (c.1820) worn by the Duchesse d'Angoulême. It was later a favorite of Empress Eugénie.

PRIVATE COLLECTION

French at Crècy in 1346 and adopted as the badge of the Prince of Wales, were a feature of court functions well into the second half of the twentieth century. With these plumes nodding behind their splendid diamond tiaras, every dowager seemed like a goddess. Since all the courts of Europe vied with one another for the palm of brilliance, few travelers went abroad without their jewelry. Frances Anne Vane Tempest Stewart, marchioness of Londonderry, appeared in 1844 before the sultan of Turkey in full court dress, blazing like the sun in a diamond tiara and feathers. On a visit to Vienna she was pleased that the empress's pearl and diamond bandeau was similar "but not so handsome" as hers, and only in Russia did she feel outshone.

Although certain elements of the Empire tiara remained in fashion—cameos and the motifs of vine leaves, grapes, laurels, Greek-key patterns, and ears of wheat—new themes were also introduced with the advent of Romanticism. J. B. Fossin, predecessor of Chaumet, revived the naturalistic designs of the eighteenth century. His success was immediate. After a ball at the Austrian embassy, *La Mode* (1830)

Alexandre Dubois Drahonnet portrait of the marchioness of Londonderry (1831) dressed for the coronation of William IV.

Fashion plate (1829) showing a ferronière falling down in a Mary Stuart point over the brow, with evening dress.

reported that "never before had stones been mounted with such finesse, elegance, and taste. The heavy combs and severe tiaras had vanished . . . while everywhere topazes, emeralds, rubies, and diamonds were ingeniously combined and set by Fossin's inimitable art to reproduce the many diverse forms of garlands, flowers, bouquets, and bowknots." His designs in the Chaumet archives were for tiaras of primroses, lilies of the valley, roses, jasmine, hawthorn, chestnut leaves, olive and ivy, and fruit, particularly cherries and red currants. A favorite Fossin motif was the bull rush, which might divide into brooches for the bodice when not required for the head. He set the flowers on trembler springs so that every movement showed them from a new and equally beautiful point of view, and for extra realism, he introduced enamel, particularly green for leaves. With hair piled high, several ornaments could be worn all together—a diamond bandeau around the head, a floral garland in the middle, and silver ears of corn in front of the comb at the back.

Another influence on tiara design was the nostalgia felt for the past. It was observed by *Les Lettres Parisiennes* (1841): "what is coming into fashion is quite simply the love, the perfect love of past times . . . in a word this year the style of the troubadour is generally adopted." This meant the *ferronière,*

Philip de Laszlo portrait of the duchess of Northumberland (1937) with the ducal strawberry leaf tiara.

DUKE OF NORTHUMBERLAND

The Northumberland strawberry leaf tiara.

DUKE OF NORTHUMBERLAND

or jeweled band centered on a specimen stone or cameo as worn by the beauties of the Renaissance. There was also the chased gold and colored gem *Bandeau Berthe*, which followed the contours of the face and was inspired by the headdress of a medieval chatelaine. Heraldry, evoking the world of chivalry, was another theme, particularly for the ducal crowns surmounted by fleurons or strawberry leaves.

In addition to a variety of design, there was a great selection of materials. There were diamonds set in silver, matt or burnished gold, filigree and cannetille, bright enamels, and colored stones—precious and semiprecious—many imported from Brazil. Coral was popular, although supplies were not always reliable, and so were seed, button, and pear pearls. Jet, cut steel, Berlin iron, onyx, and black enamel were adopted for the important category of mourning jewelry. The heroine of the novel, *A Lady of Fashion* (1856), explained why it was necessary to own not one, but several, parures of different colored gems and materials: "I cannot always be sparkling in diamonds. I must have emeralds for one style of dress, sapphire for another . . . no leader of *bon ton* can get on without all sorts and sizes of pretty gems."

Marriage, which was at that time considered to be the most important occasion in a woman's life, was marked by much solemnity, and it became customary for the bride to wear a tiara over her veil, as if at a coronation. When Princess Charlotte of Wales, heiress to the throne of England, married Prince Leopold of Saxe Coburg in 1816, she wore a magnificent silver lamé dress trimmed with Brussels point lace and, on her head, "a wreath of rose buds and leaves, composed of the most superb brilliants." Thereafter, the tiara was worn as a sign of prestige at weddings not only in England but elsewhere in Europe. When the trousseau was displayed at the reception held in the bride's home after the wedding, jewelry was also on show, and *La Mode* (1836) described the presents of a rich Parisian bride: "belt buckles, watch chains, suites of semiprecious stones, earrings, tiaras, double or triple row diamond necklaces." Thus equipped, she could take her place in society.

COURT GRANDEUR (1849–1900)

The revolution in France of 1848, which drove Louis Philippe into exile and threatened the thrones of Belgium, Austria, and Russia, did not affect England to the same extent. There, the political system was reformed by peaceful means, and the country enjoyed the twin benefits of economic prosperity and the acquisition of an empire.

At the head of the state was Queen Victoria, whose jewels were popularly regarded as an expression of national pride and prosperity. People were pleased to see the Koh-in-Noor diamond on her head at the christening of her youngest son, and, noticing she had put on her best tiara for the wedding of her eldest daughter to Prince Frederick of Prussia (1858), the newspapers said, "We feel proud." When she retreated from public life after the death of Prince Albert (1861), her son, the future Edward VII, and his wife, Alexandra, were well-suited to take her place. *Queen* (1867) reported the pageantry of a drawing room at Buckingham Palace: "The arrival of the carriages with their elaborate hammercloths, their gay liveried servants with their curled wigs, their bouquets, their cocked hats and all the glories peculiar to a Drawing Room" and inside "what struck you most was the ladies' dresses and the number and variety of the diamonds which glittered in the tiaras. . . . Those who did not wear tiaras affected large metallic gold leaves mixed with green or bunches of flowers." Again, at the state opening of Parliament, it was the richness of the feminine attire, according to *Queen*, that completed the stately picture: "The Peeresses who occupied seats in the body of the House wore plumes and displayed such magnificent parures of diamonds that it spoke well for our national prosperity. Diamond tiaras were greatly in favor and sprays of diamonds and rows of single stones were mounted on coronets and diadems of various colors to suit the rest of the costume." These tiaras were not reserved for state events, but were also brought out for balls and dinners at the town houses and country mansions of nobility. Barbara Charlton, in *Recollections of a Northumbrian Lady* (1989), recalled staying in 1852 at Alnwick Castle, home of the duke and duchess of Northumberland: "So I got busy with my diamonds for the occasion and had them mounted by Tessier in a tiara shape, a setting that has been universally admired both in England and abroad." In London, the duchess of Sutherland at Stafford House "looked an Empress with a profusion of diamonds on her head," and the duchess of Devonshire, standing at the top of the white marble staircase of Devonshire House, received her guests wearing a tall, all-round crown mounted with stones from the ancestral collection. There were some that always stood out: the "high but yet so light and handsome" tiara of the duchess of Abercorn, the Rosse emeralds, the Rossmore sapphire and pearl crown, and Lady Dudley's pearl and brilliant coronet. They added much to the interest of an evening at the Opera and gave a cachet to events such as the farewell dinner held at the Hotel Cecil before Lord Curzon left for India, when every woman present wore her tiara.

Emerald and diamond tiara of the countess of Rosse.

CHRISTIE'S

When she went abroad, the English lady did not leave her tiara at home. She needed it for diplomatic receptions on the continent and at the courts of viceroys of Ireland and of India and of the governor general of Canada, who maintained a considerable degree of state, entertaining on a lavish scale regulated by strict ceremonial. Thus they reflected the dignity, self-assurance, and splendor of the sovereign represented. This attitude prevailed not only in India, where the native tradition associated authority with princely magnificence, but also in the new colonies. Thus, from Australia, *Queen* (1866) reported that at the ball given by the mayor of Melbourne, attended by the governor general of Victoria and his wife, in token of colonial wealth and splendor "a great number of the ladies wore golden and jeweled diadems."

In France the declaration of Napoleon III as emperor, followed by his marriage with Eugénie de Montijo in 1853, brought a revival of the brilliance of the court of his uncle, Napoleon I. There were receptions twice weekly at the Tuileries, rounds of balls, dinners and concerts, gala performances at the opera, and glittering occasions at the palaces of St. Cloud, Compiègne, and Fontainebleau. The crown jewels were remodeled for the empress into matchless parures that always included a tiara. The *Illustrated London News* (1867) was impressed by "her magnificent and dazzling headdress" at a Tuileries Ball: "In the midst of a tiara of diamond shone the Regent, 140 carats in weight, and on each side of it, as if to show off its untarnished water, shone sprays of black diamonds." She was well supported by the women members of the Bonaparte family, especially by the emperor's cousin, Princess Mathilde Demidoff, of whom it was said that her high and noble forehead seemed to have been made for a tiara. The court set the pattern followed by the wives of the nobility, of diplomats, of bankers, and of industrialists. *Queen* (1862) reported in a Paris letter, "for evening, ladies will adorn their heads regally. Every woman will have the air of an empress, diadems and tiaras for grand toilettes will be obligatory."

With the fall of the Second Empire in 1870 and the establishment of the Third Republic, the tiara disappeared from Parisian official receptions. In his history *Les Bijoux Anciens et Modernes* (1887), Eugène Fontenay observed that "since the tiara was hardly compatible with government by a republic, women made do with elaborate combs and floral aigrettes instead." In private, however, such was the wealth concentrated on Paris that displays of luxury and privilege continued. At a concert given by Princess Bibesco, *Queen* (1872) noticed the diamond and pink coral tiara of the countess de Gramedo and the viscountess de Tredern in white brocade embroidered with irises, her hair crowned with a Greek-key pattern diamond band bordered by two rows of diamonds, "forming a splendid diadem."

Elsewhere in Europe, from Lisbon to St. Petersburg, court life flourished, and each royal family had important jewelry. Immense care was taken to see that when daughters married they had the right type of ornament for their royal duties. From Germany, Empress Frederick wrote to her daughter, Sophie, queen of Greece, "I'm sure you looked a duck with your turquoise diadem and the turquoises round your little neck for the dinner and circle on the Independence Day." The two leading Viennese jewelers, Bussler and Köchert, proved their mastery of the Habsburg grand manner by the splendor of the tiaras made for the beautiful Empress Elizabeth and the archduchesses. Ironically, these magnificent creations belong to the final years of the dynasty, whose rule had begun in the thirteenth century. It was the same in Russia, where the house of Romanoff was also doomed, and yet the cult of magnificence flourished as never before. In Queen Margherita, wife of Umberto I, Italy had a sovereign with a true air of majesty, a great collection of tiaras appropriate for the variety of events she attended, and her example did much to encourage the ladies of the Roman, Florentine, and Milanese nobility to display their jewels. King Umberto's sister, Queen Maria Pia of Portugal, also gave a lead to the ladies of her court, using the unrivaled state collection of diamonds mined in Brazil for a series of new tiaras from the best makers of Lisbon and Paris. The most extraordinary was the star tiara from Estevao de Sousa consisting of twenty-five graduated five-pointed stars mounted on tremblers, which quivered incessantly and cast forth a continuous sparkle of light around her head.

These twilight years for so many monarchies proved a golden age for the jewelers. Their stands at the international exhibitions, held at intervals from 1851 to 1900, drew the largest crowds, and pride of place was always given to a tiara. The heraldic tiara exhibited by the French jeweler Lemonnier at the exhibition held at the Crystal Palace in London, and bought for the queen of Spain, affirmed the continuing importance of this theme. Some were indicative of rank, particularly the ducal strawberry leaves, but others represented national emblems—the rose, shamrock, and thistle of England, Ireland, and Scotland—and family badges such as the oak leaves of the Howards, the holly of the Drummonds, and the knot of the Staffords. Princesses of the royal house of Bourbon and those women loyal to them often chose the fleur-de-lis motif: it inspired the imposing ruby and diamond tiara created by Köchert of Vienna for the wife of Ferdinand of Bulgaria, Princess Maria Luisa of Parma (1887). In Italy, the Savoy knot from the collar of the Order of the Annunciation was adopted for jewelry, including tiaras.

The art of the past continued to provide a quarry of ideas. Köchert's pearl and diamond "Byzantine" tiara was the showpiece of his stand at the international exhibition held in Vienna (1873), and the Renaissance was the source of the design of the Devonshire parure made by C. F. Hancock of London (1856). The naturalistic rococo styles were more popular than ever, though of all the flowers created in metal and precious stones, there seems to have been a preference for the wild rose and the daisy. Another favorite was the ivy leaf, which Köchert took as the motif for the great emerald and diamond parure ordered by the emperor Franz Joseph for the empress Elizabeth to mark their twenty-fifth wedding anniversary (1879). Equally characteristic of the rococo style was the shell tiara, of which the most outstanding example, exhibited by Mellerio at the Paris International Exhibition (1867), was bought by the queen of Spain as a wedding present for her daughter, the Infanta Marie Isabelle. The curved wide shell

Philip de Laszlo portrait of the queen of Bulgaria (1894) wearing a fleur-de-lis tiara made for her by Köchert of Vienna.

Princess Stéphanie of Belgium, of Bourbon descent, wears a fleur-de-lis tiara and other jewels created for her by Joseph Chaumet at the time of her marriage to Elemer, Count Lonyay, in 1908. She was first married to Archduke Rudoph of Austria, who died at Mayerling under mysterious circumstances.

Photograph advertising the stand of C. F. Hancock at the Vienna International Exhibition in 1873. The model is wearing a peacock tiara.

entirely pavéd with diamonds was hung with seven pearls and eighteen briolettes, which shook and scintillated with every movement.

The return to classical design was stimulated in France by Napoleon III with his purchase of the Campana collection of ancient Greek and Roman jewelry for the Louvre in 1861. As a result, tiaras of Greek-key pattern, laurel wreaths, ears of corn, honeysuckle, and palmettes worn low on the brow in imitation of Empress Josephine came into fashion again. However, the outstanding exponent of the archaeological style of jewelry was the firm of Castellani in Rome, directed by Fortunato Pio Castellani (1794–1864) and then by his son Augusto (1829–1914). Using the techniques of the ancient Etruscan and Roman craftsmen, they quickly gained an international reputation, especially among people of artistic and intellectual tastes. Deeply patriotic, the Castellani were supporters of the Risorgimento, as were some of their customers, one of whom appeared at a London dinner party in 1865 with a golden wreath of laurel on her head and the tricolor sash of the united Italy tied across her white dress.

The majority of tiaras were mounted with diamonds, owing to the discovery of the mines of South Africa in the late 1860s, which released more of these stones than ever before into the market. This coincided with the introduction of electric light, which suited the glitter and sparkle of diamonds on the head. So many women were now wearing tiaras that they could be ordered by mail from the London Association of Diamond Merchants. Customers resident in the country could choose from catalogues in which each design was drawn to size, with the stones numbered and the price clearly stated. Observing this phenomenon, the *Illustrated London News* (1898) concluded that "the quantity of jewels worn by women at all the smart evening parties seems to indicate that the world grows richer every week. Hereditary gems are even outshone by tiaras of no ancestry whatsoever and the young married woman who does not glitter and scintillate at all points is the exception rather than the rule."

Gold archaeological-style laurel tiara (c.1860).

RICHARD DIGBY, LONDON

Absolutism stood firm in Russia during the second half of the nineteenth century, allowing the rich to indulge in displays of luxury eclipsing all other nations. Their palatial homes with spacious halls, immense windows, marble walls and columns, malachite vases, and shining parquet floors made wonderful settings for Paris gowns and jewelry. Some women kept their collections in glass cases on show in their bedrooms, guarded by icons of the Virgin and St. Nicolas, with a lamp burning in front. They took care to match their dresses to the color of each parure—mauve with amethysts, rubies with pink, sapphires with blue; the size of the stones and the profusion in which they were worn was beyond anything seen in western Europe. When dressed in the picturesque court dress that derived from the national costume, the ladies looked almost medieval. The amply cut velvet robe was heavily embroidered in silver, gold, or in every color of the rainbow and worn over a white satin underskirt with a long train attached and wide hanging sleeves. The *kokoshnik,* which was worn over a veil and gave every woman the appearance of being crowned, was not universally becoming, according to the traveler Marquis de Custine (1841): "Very ancient, it gives an air of nobleness and originality to handsome persons whilst it singularly enhances the ugliness of the plain ones. Unfortunately these are very numerous at the Russian court." It inspired two distinctive forms of tiara: the halo, with surface either open or filled in, and the fringe, "spike," or sun-ray design. These were worn not only by Russian women but were also widely adopted abroad. With immense means at their disposal, Russian grand duchesses could order the grandest "fenders" mounted with splendid stones not only from the St. Petersburg jewelers Keibel, Fabergé, and Bolin, but also from Cartier and Chaumet.

D. Asikrimov photograph (1900) of Grand Duchess Elizabeth Feodorovna, sister of the Tsarina, wife of Grand Duke Serge, Governor of Moscow, wearing a halo-shaped *kokoshnik* studded with cabochon stones over her veil.

SOTHEBY'S

Never had so many tiaras been seen as in the first decade of the twentieth century, and *Tatler* (1909) reported that, formerly reserved for royalty, for the wives of wealthy peers and ambassadresses, the "tiara was now worn on all sorts of unsuitable occasions. Nowadays one sees them at the play, at small parties, and at dinner in restaurants. Then the modern bride expects at least a couple of tiaras among her wedding presents and four or five are sometimes seen at smart marriages. There is the story of the woman who returned to London after some time away and found that even those marrying on an income of £500 a year expected a tiara."

For Edward VII, who had the grand manner of a modern Louis XIV, every woman wore her best dress and most beautiful jewels. Thus, during his reign, the coronation of 1902, the court balls, state openings of Parliament, and gala performances at the opera brought out the most gorgeous display of tiaras, which were noticed more than any other jewel. It was the same at the great country houses. When King Edward and Queen Alexandra stayed with the duke and duchess of Devonshire, *Queen* (1906) reported, "the dresses worn by the guests were all the newest and smartest, and several of the women had brought down their jewels, some of which had never been seen before, only having been recovered from the hands of the jewelers just before the owners themselves started for Chatsworth. Consuelo, duchess of Marlborough, had a magnificent crown of diamonds set in the French fashion even outshining the beautiful and well-known crown which the duchess of Devonshire wears on very big occasions."

What was this new French fashion in tiaras? It meant lighter, more graceful, and more delicate designs executed in platinum, which could be wrought as fine as lace, and which Cartier had introduced in 1896. Louis Cartier said that whereas the thick and heavy gold and silver settings were like the armor of jewelry, the new platinum was like embroidery. Once jewelers had mastered the technical problems of making the light and thin metal sufficiently strong enough to support quantities of gems, they could transform the appearance of jewelry, reducing settings to a minimum, giving the fullest value to the splendor of great collet stones and to those in the surrounding scrolls. There was an invasion of London by the Parisian jewelers, who from 1902 began the process of resetting family gems into new tiaras for the coronation, which continued over the decade, reaching another climax in 1911 for the coronation of George V. Queen Alexandra was so impressed by a sapphire and diamond tiara worn by an American in London that she decided to have her own stones reset by the same Parisian jeweler. Other well-known tiaras that represented the new fashion were the emerald and diamond crown of the countess of Warwick, "remarkable for its exquisite Cartier setting," Lady Anson's diamond-and-pearl tiara set "à la Cartier very lightly in platinum," and the duchess of Westminster's high, all-round diamond crown. Some were exhibited for charity by Cartier just before the coronation in 1911 with others of remarkable design. Of these the most outstanding were the duchess of Newcastle's superb wide band of scrolls surmounted by a tall feather all executed in large diamonds (c. 1820) and the yellow diamond "feather tiara of Lady Galway which is entirely composed of diamond feathers carried right round the head." Although the all-round crown was the most up-to-date fashion, so as not to be seen in the same tiara too often, those who could afford to do so had several to choose from: the duchess of Westminster had no fewer than five, as did the countess of Dudley and Lady Tullibardine. Lady Powis, unable to choose which one to wear to the opera, took both and changed from one to the other in the interval. The duchess of Wellington, whose all-round crown was famous, arranged to wear her second best as a stomacher covering the front of her bodice.

The increase in the number of occasions to which tiaras were worn, and the number of women who owned them, coincided with the coiffure à la Pompadour, which not only made a firm foundation for the ornament but was also extremely flattering to most women, with the hair puffed out at the sides as well as dressed high. This style was almost universally adopted by the guests attending the wedding of Princess Daisy of Connaught to the crown prince of Sweden (1905) held in the shadow of Windsor Castle in the historic St. George's Chapel. Everyone was in full evening dress, and the blaze of the diamonds in the tiaras was softened by the arrangement of the hair. As always, much publicity was given to the wedding presents, and pictures of the jewelry of Princess Daisy were accorded two pages in the *Illustrated London News*. When the heir to the duke of Sutherland married, the tiara he had designed especially for his bride, Eileen, made a great impression on *Queen* (1912): "Very wide on the brow, it was formed of one deep bandeau as it were with an outer ring of great diamonds compassing the entire head. Within this, again was an exquisite 'filling in' design of brilliants, the whole finished off with another 'ring' of great diamonds while topping the whole in front were three feathers like branches of the same lovely stones giving height to the whole crown."

The accession of George V with his wife, Queen Mary, in 1911 brought to the throne one of the most avid collectors of jewelry of all time. She is said to have worn a tiara even when dining alone at

Newcastle tiara (c. 1820) exhibited at Cartier, London, 1911.

CHRISTIE'S

Princess Henckel von Donnersmarck (1895) wearing jewels made for her by Joseph Chaumet.

PRINCE GUIDOTTO HENCKEL VON DONNERSMARCK

night, and no jewelry ever meant more to her. When her aunt, the grand duchess of Mecklenbourg Strelitz celebrated her ninetieth birthday, Queen Mary urged her: "If you have a dinner to celebrate, you must wear your pearl and diamond tiara with your English orders." Certainly tiaras played an important role in German court life, and each great family, such as the Thurn and Taxis, possessed several, some family heirlooms, others newly commissioned from Robert Koch in Frankfurt, Köchert in Austria, or from Paris. Romantic and princely tiaras were bought from Chaumet by two very good German customers, the princess Henckel von Donnersmarck and the Baron de Courlande, both prominent in Berlin society. Meanwhile, the wives and daughters of the old French aristocracy continued to wear the tiara, in circumstances described by Marcel Proust in his novel *Remembrance of Things Past:* "Just like a Queen holding her circle," the Duchesse de Guermantes, first lady of Parisian society, looked "splendid in her emerald and diamond tiara with pink dress with a long train." At each Rothschild wedding, tiaras were put on show with the other jewelry in the wedding casket: Noémi Halphen received no fewer than six when she married Maurice de Rothschild (1907). Similarly, women members of the rich financial dynasties of Stern, Fould, Gunzbourg, and Cahen d'Anvers, of the Protestant bankers Lehideux, Mallet, Hottinguer, and de Pourtalès, and the industrialists Wendel and Schneider, acquired superb jewels including tiaras.

Since Paris led, the other jewelers copied designs originating in that city. The most successful designs derived from the art of the Louis XV and Louis XVI periods, which lent themselves particularly well to the setting of diamonds and colored stones. At least one of the six tiaras given to Baroness Maurice de Rothschild as wedding presents was in this style: the emeralds and diamonds, according to *Les Modes* (1907), were "mounted to wonderful effect: in an exquisite Louis XVI design." These eighteenth-century revivals were principally the trellis, or *résille*, shell, flowers, bullrushes, ribbons, bowknots, festoons, tassels, and fringes. The classical motifs—laurel and olive wreaths, running scrolls of vine and acanthus, ears of wheat and oat husks, palmettes, honeysuckle, volutes, and Greek-key pattern—took a new lease on life.

Because of the social significance of the tiara, many women reserved their best stones for it. These stones were shown to particular advantage standing up high above a plain circlet, linked together by festoons, or swinging freely within a series of arcades. One of Cartier's greatest successes was the design

Lady Galway (1902) wearing the feather tiara exhibited by Cartier in London, 1911.

Princely marriage at Windsor from
L'Illustration (1905).

of interlaced circles from which a customer, such as Countess Hohenfelsen, might hang either her collection of pear-shaped diamonds or her pearls (1911). Joseph Chaumet's waterfall or fountain design, first made in 1894, and his stalactite tiara, with briolettes dripping from frozen icicles, showed off the brilliance and sparkle of diamonds to magical effect.

Just before the outbreak of World War I, there were signs that this great period for the tiara was coming to an end. According to the *Illustrated London News* (1913), there were fewer great entertainments than before: "For one reason or another several of the best houses in town have not been opened to receive guests at all and there has been a vast increase in taxation which reduces means." *Queen* (1913), reporting a ball at the town house of the marchioness of Zetland, noticed the men in their orders, and was surprised to see women in tiaras "which are so seldom seen these days." This was because the bandeau, or flat, jeweled fillet binding the hair, was becoming increasingly fashionable. *Les Modes* (1912) predicted, "This winter the diamond tiara will be replaced by the narrow bandeau which goes all round the head." One of the first to discard her tiara was the ultrachic baroness de Meyer, and thereafter the bandeau, worn with very long earrings, enjoyed great success. The narrow dimensions did not leave much room for ornament: the most popular motifs were the neoclassical Greek key and honeysuckle and light foliage interspersed with collet stones. Inspired by moiré silk, Cartier created a trompe l'oeil bandeau reproducing the shimmer in diamonds on a black ground: this was bought by Princess Antoine Bibesco (1910). Some bandeaux were combined with a holder for feathers and might be combined with a jeweled aigrette. This last, which was immensely popular, was one of the first jewels to respond to the influence of Islamic and Chinese art.

THE TWENTIETH CENTURY II (1918-2000)

The history of the tiara between the armistice of 1918 and the end of the twentieth century can be divided into two parts—the period terminating with the outbreak of World War II in 1939 and the half century that followed the peace of 1945. In view of the great social and economic changes that have taken place during that time, it may seem odd that the tiara has not been consigned to oblivion, but many hereditary ones have survived, and new designs, more compatible with contemporary fashions in hair styles and dress, have been created for official and private formal events.

The lead has come from England, where Queen Mary, wife of George V, Queen Elizabeth, their daughter-in-law, and Queen Elizabeth II have worn their splendid tiaras for all important occasions. The first sign that the tiara was not to be relinquished after the war years was a report in *Tatler* (1919): "Diamond tiaras we'd almost forgotten the existence of, but whether there's revolutions ahead or not, some of us are evidently determined the gay times shall come back again, for two American Duchesses and some more friends combined to give a rather lovely scroll design to the future Lady Albermarle." The first state balls, in honor of the visits of the king and queen of the Belgians (1921) and of the king and queen of Italy (1924), had hostesses such as Mrs. Greville entertaining again, although many had moved out of their ancestral town mansions. The *Illustrated London News* (1922), observing how many women were wearing tiaras at state functions, approved: "The tiara is a much derided ornament, yet it is a characteristic one of British great ladies and it is worn by eight out of ten of them with dignity and imposing effect." At the Italian ball that Mrs. Greville held in her Charles Street house for the state visit, according to *Tatler* (1924), "She, gowned in pale green embroidered in gold thread, was wearing her big Cartier tiara which was carried out in platinum in the favourite Empire shape." Only the display at the state openings of Parliament reflected the political unrest and succession of strikes culminating in the general strike of 1926: *Tatler* (1924) reported that the women present "were not wearing their best dresses and jewels, due to nervousness about the political situation." The marchioness of Londonderry, who kept the flag flying, continued to hold her receptions for one thousand guests on the eve of each state opening as splendidly bejeweled as her predecessors had been in the magnificent family diamonds.

Tiaras were worn to new forms of entertaining, particularly the charity ball, to private parties given by "new money," and, as always, to the opera. They were regarded as a glamorous accessory to evening dress. In an article on weddings, *Vogue* (1921) affirmed that the day of the tiara was by no means past: "after the engagement ring the tiara is the most thrilling topic of conversation not only in the mounting, but in the choice of stones which depend on the type of woman." The ledgers of the Parisian jewelers record tiaras specially commissioned for brides: Prince Alexander Murat bought a magnificent diamond-and-pearl scrollwork design for Yvonne Gillois from Chaumet (1922), and the future earl of Carnarvon had the family diamonds reset into a new tiara for Catherine Wendell the same year. Others were bought by Spanish, Italian, Belgian, and South and North American customers.

Diamond and hanging pearl
tiara worn by the duchess of
Marlborough, who acquired it at
the sale of Russian crown jewels
held at Christie's in 1927.

CHRISTIE'S

Many seemed to prefer traditional designs—laurel wreaths, vine and acanthus scroll, bow-knots, and sprays of leaves and flowers—in the eighteenth-century tradition. Gladys Deacon, who married the duke of Marlborough after his divorce from Consuelo Vanderbilt, chose an antique design of great beauty from the Russian state jewels sold by the Soviets at Christie's in 1927, for her party at Carlton House Terrace, where she wore "on the top of her head the famous tiara of diamonds and hanging pearls with a lovely peacock blue gown from Louise Boulanger."

Meanwhile, jewelers thought of ways to rejuvenate the tiara, and *Vogue* (1921) declared, "Gone are the days of the heavy tiara: simplicity in jewelery as in dress is ahead of us." With the new fashion in dress—short, straight, sleeveless, and tunic-like—went the modern hair style, cropped like a boy's, drawn back from the forehead. Besides being compatible with this fashionable silhouette, the tiara now had to conform to the artistic style that crystallized at the time of the *Exposition des Arts Décoratifs*, which opened in Paris in 1925. This meant severely geometric outlines, contrasts of color, mixtures of stone cuts, and combinations of both opaque and transparent gems. Instead of finding inspiration from the art of eighteenth-century France, jewelers looked to more exotic places. *Vogue* (1925) reported that "many nations contributed rare designs for jewels . . . Persian and Turkish are much in use and there are also the Chinese patterns of numberless stones all variously designed and suggesting the ancient Chinese miniatures of 100 colors. Oriental designs have been worn often in recent years by many dark-haired women of southern beauty."

Exemplifying the Art Deco tiara are two designs from Chaumet. For Lady Wimborne, a famous London political hostess, Chaumet created a severely geometric design executed in rubies and diamonds rising to a point over the brow, a design which was repeated soon after for the grand duchess of Luxembourg, centering on a large cabochon emerald. Mauboussin made a tiara of the fountain motif

Cecil Beaton photograph (1925) of Lady Wimborne in her ruby-and-diamond tiara and other Chaumet jewelry.

SOTHEBY'S

using diamonds of different cuts to simulate the play of water. Cartier's Bérènice tiara, shown at the *Exposition des Arts Décoratifs*, was in the severe geometric shape rising to a peak and filled with rows of melon-cut Indian emeralds, of uneven size, terminating at each end with an Egyptian lotus flower. The model on the stand wore it, Empire fashion, low on the brow. The bandeau, which was also worn in this way, was now made of overlapping discs or *écus comptés*, braiding and geometric motifs, but still wrought in platinum and as supple as silk. Every "dream jewel case" of the 1920s contained a bandeau as well as a tiara, for not only were bandeaux easy to wear, but they were often convertible to bracelets and could be clasped round the neck.

This creative period came to an abrupt end with the stock market crash of October 1929. Since few people could afford luxuries, many jewelers went out of business. Only the occasional wedding with royalty, such as that of Barbara Hutton to Prince Midvani (1933), provided the stimulus for new designs and for resetting family stones, as was the case with Chaumet's commissions for the Spanish marriages in Rome (1935) and that of Prince Alfonso de Bourbon in Vienna (1936). *Vogue* was impressed by the "taste and sumptuosity" of these designs, which so happily blended tradition and modernism. Uncompromisingly new, Van Cleef excelled with the abstract tiara and necklace executed in diamonds of different cuts ordered by Queen Nazli for the marriage of her daughter, Princess Fawzia, to the Shah of Iran (1938).

The most important revival was in London when the Silver Jubilee of George V was celebrated followed by the coronation of George VI in 1937. *Vogue* (1935) observed: "Have you noticed lately that tiaras are absolutely the rage? Every woman wears one on the slightest provocation and they always seem to look their best in them." Family tiaras with matchless stones and new ones appeared at ceremonies in Westminster Abbey, at the court ball, at grand receptions, and at banquets held for the visitors

Cecil Beaton photograph (c.1937)
of the duchess of Buccleuch
wearing her hereditary jewels for
the coronation of George VI.

Molly Bishop drawing of the
duchess of Buccleuch (1973)
wearing a jeweled belt from
the 1830s as a tiara.

who came from all over the world. "Chips" Channon recorded in his *Diaries* the jewels displayed at the duchess of Sutherland's ball: "Every woman blazed with diamonds, the duchess of Sutherland in her reset family tiara, the Marchioness of Londonderry, the Countess of Haddington in their high 'fenders,' the Begum Aga Khan with her emeralds and diamonds, Princess Paul of Yugoslavia in sky blue and huge diamond tiara, the Grand Duchess of Hesse in pink and silver lamé dress with spiked, all-round diamond crown." Later, at Lady Howard de Walden's ball at Seaford House, he saw "a gorgeous cavalcade of our best tiaras moving up London's most effective staircase." Present at the grand gala at Covent Garden of the state visit of President and Madame Lebrun, he was proud of "our London beauties literally covered with jewels . . . half the women wore tiaras. It was a brave sight." Other "tiara occasions" were diplomatic receptions, coming-out balls in country houses, hunt balls, and dances held in aid of charities such as the Red Cross. The new tiaras were in tune with the slender lines of the fashionable evening dresses and with the soft curls of the more feminine coiffure of the 1930s, yet remained formal and dignified. *Vogue* (1937) liked "the happy combination of the grace and grandeur of the Belle Epoque with the added elegance and chic of modern workmanship." This still meant platinum mounts, but now reduced to the very lightest of skeletons, and stones cut to new shapes—moon, oblong, square, and round. While "all-white" designs with diamonds or diamonds and pearls were the most common, sapphires, emeralds, and rubies were also introduced in combination with them, and to striking effect. Color was also provided by coral and semi-precious stones, particularly slabs of golden topazes and aquamarines, which had the advantage of being inexpensive, an important consideration during the aftermath of the stock market crash. Motifs varied from the traditional sun rays, stars, arcades, laurel, flower patterns, and feathers, to the Egyptian lotus, to spirals and abstract forms echoing contemporary architecture. An unusual design exhibited by Cartier at the Exposition Coloniale (1931) was inspired by the crown worn by temple dancers in Thailand. They were worn differently now, as halos, standing up the back of the head, blazing with light or flashing with color.

For the second time in this century, formal entertaining and displays of magnificence were brought to an end by a world war, declared in 1939. Tiaras were hidden away once again, and, as far as England was concerned, did not reappear until 1947 when the future Elizabeth II married Philip Mountbatten, duke of Edinburgh. The bride received gifts of jewelry, including tiaras, and among the festivities a grand reception was held at Buckingham Palace. Queen Elizabeth and Queen Mary both wore their best tiaras, and so did Queen Ena of Spain, Queen Alexandra of Yugoslavia, Queen Ingrid of Denmark, and Princess Juliana of Holland, as well as others among the thousand guests present at this historic occasion. It signaled the end of austerity, and for Jacques Dumaine, who accompanied President Auriol on his state visit to England (1950), there was "an enchanted atmosphere in the great rooms once more and Queen Victoria's world has come back as if by magic thanks to the brilliance of the tiaras and

The Grand Duchess of Hesse with
her star tiara (1934).

full dress decorations . . . for the past two years we have been longing to see this old world luxury again." On the return visit to Paris (1957) it was felt that the spectacle inside the Paris opera house could not compare with that of London, for the fine heirloom jewels and tiaras of the old British families were missing. Even critics of British fashion such as Lady Pamela Berry acknowledged that "for the grand and glittering occasion the English woman who was not afraid to get her jewels out of the bank looked best . . . when the most distinguished French women, in their starkly simple dresses, with few jewels, are surrounded by English women whose tiaras blazed and dazzled, it is at these that one looks." Nancy Mitford, in *Harper's Bazaar* (1952), agreed: "There is no more dazzling sight in the world than a ball at Buckingham Palace." There were many such occasions, more state visits, more balls for weddings, notably those for Princess Alexandra with Angus Ogilvy (1963) and for Prince Charles with Lady Diana Spencer (1981). Lady Jebb, wife of the ambassador to Paris (1954–60), who always wore a tiara when she attended these events, was interested in the tiaras worn by foreign royalty in exile, which she thought eclipsed those of families still reigning. There was a distinct falling off at the state opening of Parliament, which few attended during the long years of Labor government; those who did wore their second or third best dresses. The election of Edward Heath, which brought the Conservatives back to power in 1970, was welcomed by a revival of the former grandeur, and the peeresses turned up in the most wonderful clothes and jewels to show their relief at a respite from socialism. Now that the new Labor government intends to abolish the hereditary peers, all this brilliant pageantry is condemned to oblivion.

What has always impressed foreigners is not just the display of splendor at state openings, Buckingham Palace, Windsor Castle, the lord mayor's banquets, and other official events, but at private houses. During the past fifty years, there have been coming-of-age balls for the sons and daughters of grand country estates with invitations clearly stating "tiaras will be worn." Those who owned them took them out from the bank, those who did not either borrowed or bought new ones. Most recently, Maureen,

Lady Jebb at the Paris embassy wearing her mother's ivy leaf tiara (1957).

THE ILLUSTRATED LONDON NEWS PICTURE LIBRARY

The queen of Spain and Princess del Drago at a party in Rome (1954).

THE ILLUSTRATED LONDON NEWS PICTURE LIBRARY

marchioness of Dufferin and Ava, celebrated her ninetieth birthday with a ball at Claridge's Hotel at which she wore the family shamrock tiara, and many of her guests wore theirs, thus creating a very special atmosphere. As for weddings, the custom of the bride wearing a tiara continues, and almost every British one pictured in this book has been used in this way during the past fifty years.

It is the same elsewhere in Europe, where the tiara is seen at all grand weddings in Spain, Portugal, France, the Netherlands, Austria, Italy, and the Scandinavian countries, with guests bringing their own tiaras to wear at the festivities. Yet there has been a change. In France, whereas the inauguration of the theater at the Chateau de Groussay (1957) and parties held at the Hotel Lambert and the Chateau de Méry during the 1950s and 1960s were attended by women in Dior gowns and tiaras, all duly photographed by *Vogue*, this is no longer so. During the same period in Italy, when a princely Roman family such as Pallavicini or Torlonia gave a coming-out ball for a daughter, pictures of the guests with their jewels would appear in the press, but nowadays such reports are rare. Events of this kind are kept strictly private, because it is felt politically and fiscally imprudent to be seen to live in a grand manner. There is also the problem of security that worsens every year, accompanied by a rise in the costs of insurance. According to one distinguished French owner of a tiara with valuable stones, the cost of hiring armed outriders to escort her car to a party at Versailles was less than the insurance premium.

Nonetheless, the process of resetting old stones into new tiaras has continued, although in England it has never again reached the peak of 1953, when Queen Elizabeth II was crowned at Westminster Abbey. The main demand ever since has come from the Middle East, where the inborn love of splendor is matched by colossal fortunes based on oil. Wonderful tiaras have been created by Harry Winston for the Iranian royal family, including the glorious multicolored diamond tiara worn by Empress Farah when she married Muhammed Reza Shah (1958). Other masterpieces of modern jewelry were designed by Van Cleef for the Shah's coronation (1967). For the king of Morocco, who bought parures at regular intervals from Chaumet, a tiara was always included. It is the same for many other customers, most of whom prefer to remain anonymous.

Whereas in the past the tiara—particularly the great hereditary "fender"—was an assertion of rank and wealth, now, except for special royal commissions, it is the decorative value that counts most. Important stones, such as the Arcot diamonds, which once shone out from the Westminster tiara, are now mounted as earrings, in necklaces, or often in rings. To suit modern hair styles and evening dress, designs have to be light and understated, and the chief glory is in the collection of stones, blazing out in the very latest cuts. The most recent talent to have met the challenge of the tiara is Joel Rosenthal (JAR of Paris), widely regarded as the most creative of the new generation of jewelers who have emerged in the final decades of this century. American born, he brings a fresh approach to this most symbolic ornament.

At first sight it might seem strange that the tiara, symbolic of hereditary rank and privilege, should be adopted by citizens of a republic whose constitution is enshrined around the principle that "all men are created equal." Yet over the past two hundred years, tiaras have been worn with ease and distinction by American women, not only those married to diplomats and to European titles, but as hostesses and guests at formal events on both sides of the Atlantic.

During the first half of the nineteenth century, wealthy Americans were already outvying the English residents in French society, because, as Edward Bulwer Lytton put it in his novel *The Parisians* (1873), "they spend more money, their men speak French better, the women are better dressed, and as a general rule, have read more largely and converse more frankly." An early social success was Colonel Thorn, who enlisted the help of the Princesse de Béthune and comtesse de Rohan Chabot, whom he met at the fashionable spa of Baden Baden. They agreed to give him a list of good Parisian society provided he invited no Americans and dropped his old friends. He took their advice, rented a fine old mansion from the sister of Louis Philippe, then ruler of France, and entertained splendidly. Three Thorn daughters married into the French aristocracy—the comtesse de Varaigne, the baronne de Pierres, future lady-in-waiting to the empress Eugènie, and the comtesse de Ferrusac—and a son married the sister-in-law of Prince Klemens Metternich, the Austrian statesman. Mrs. Thorn and her daughters not only dressed well but wore the jewelry then fashionable, which included tiaras, recorded in the Chaumet/Fossin archives. The most important were a wreath of diamond oak leaves (1839) and, for baronne de Pierres, an all-round crown of ducal strawberry leaves, and a diamond-and-black enamel bandeau (1842). Also resident in Paris then was the French-born Marie Charlotte Louise Bingham, whose husband, William, represented the Philadelphia banking family: she, too, was a customer of Chaumet/Fossin, from whom she bought a diamond garland of flowers, buds, and leaves (1837); a chased gold, colored stone, diamond-and-pearl

Diamond tiara (1917) of Lady Decies
by Cartier.

SOTHEBY'S

Photograph of Lady Decies,
formerly Elizabeth Drexel, widow of
Harry Lehr, wearing her Cartier tiara
with court dress.

PRIVATE COLLECTION

Gothic-style bandeau (1839); and another, more important garland, called a "Mancini," composed of twin bouquets falling down like showers against the cheeks and culminating in diamond fringes. Mrs. Greene, also married to a banker in Paris, bought one of the diamond wreaths, while the French-born Mrs. Henry Livingston II, on a visit, acquired no fewer than three tiaras, one of them part of a turquoise-and-diamond parure with matching necklace and earrings.

After the Civil War, improved rail and steamer services brought more Americans to Paris, and there were many who chose to reside there, enjoying freedom from personal taxation and the hospitality of Emperor Napoleon III and his wife, the Empress Eugènie. Invitations to the balls and receptions at the Tuileries were readily available, and favorites of the empress, such as the Boston-born Lillie Moulton, married to the banker Charles Moulton (later de Hegermann Lindencrone), were entertained in house parties at the palaces of Fontainebleau and Compiègne. Just as the ladies of the imperial court wore crinolined dresses from Worth, fine jewels, and tiaras, so, too, did the American guests. After 1870, even though the fall of the Second Empire deprived France of the brilliance of a court life, Paris continued to attract more and more Americans intent on enjoying themselves. New, comfortable hotels were built for visitors, culminating in the opening of the Ritz in the Place Vendôme in 1898, near the famous dressmakers and jewelers of the Rue de la Paix. Permanent members of what Henry James called the "American encampment en plein Paris" were Mrs. Bell, sister of James Gordon Bennett, proprietor of the *New York Herald Tribune*; Mrs. Meredith Howland, granddaughter of Commodore Vanderbilt; and Mrs. Ridgeway. Like Colonel Thorn before them, they made their mark on Parisian society and equipped themselves for the part with expensive tiaras. In the interwar period, their place was taken by Mrs. Harry Lehr (later Lady Decies), for whom Cartier made a splendid laurel crown tiara (1917), and the decorator, Elsie de Wolfe, who, at the age of seventy, was nominated one of the "world's best dressed women." She celebrated by dyeing her hair blue to match her new aquamarine spiral-pattern tiara from Cartier.

By the turn of the century some of the grandest French families had gilded their shields afresh with new gold through marriages with the daughters of the American captains of industry and finance. The way was led by Marie-Elizabeth Forbes and the Duke de Choiseul Praslin in 1874, followed by Alice Heine and the Duke de Richelieu in 1875, Laura Montgomery with Count Otto de Pourtalès in 1891, Helen Barbey with Count Herman de Pourtalès in 1891, Mattie Elizabeth Mitchell with the Duke del Rochefoucauld in 1892, and Anna Gould with Marquis Boni de Castellane in 1895. The latter, who had excellent taste, described in his *Confessions* (1924) how Anna looked on her first appearance in Parisian society: "radiant and girlish in spangled white muslin, her slim waist encircled by a rose red sash, and in her dark hair she wore a wreath of diamond leaves made by the famous jeweler, Aucoc." She had other tiaras, too: a pair of diamond-and-emerald Valkyrie wings and a bandeau hung with a large briolette diamond in the center, both from Chaumet, and a second wreath of laurel, this one from Cartier (1903).

One of the most original tiaras created for American-born wives of French noblemen was the diamond bandeau surmounted by Valkyrie wings shimmering with briolettes of Princess Edmond de Polignac, daughter of Isaac Singer, the sewing machine millionaire, and a great enthusiast of Wagnerian opera. Although never as numerous as before World War I, tiaras continued to be bought by Americans married to French noblemen throughout the rest of the twentieth century. The Boston-born Baroness Hottinguer ordered a diamond oak leaf crown bandeau from Chaumet (1920), and Lady Granard purchased one for her daughter Moira upon her marriage to Count Louis de Brantes in 1935. Grace Kelly, who married Prince Rainier of Monaco in 1956, wore tiaras from Van Cleef & Arpels at all her official engagements.

There were even more marriages between American heiresses and English aristocrats, since London, with its parks, its palaces, and social life centered on a stable monarchy had more attractions than any other European capital. For Antony Trollope in his novel *He Knew He Was Right* (1869), Miss Carry Spalding from the United States was suited to be the wife of Lord Peterborough, because, "she has just the brow for a coronet." According to *Queen*, these Anglo-American marriages began with Helen Magruder and Lord Abinger in 1863, followed by Juliet Warden and Sir William Carrington in 1871, Jennie Jerome with Lord Randolph Churchill (parents of the statesman Winston Churchill) in 1874, Consuelo Yznaga and the future duke of Manchester in 1876, and Mary Reade and Viscount Falkland in 1879. In 1903 *Lady's Realm* estimated that at least twenty-seven such alliances had been contracted. Tiaras were essential for court presentations, the state opening of Parliament, and at the opera, as well as many other formal events, and those of the American duchesses were particularly striking. Outstanding was the diamond crown given by her father to Consuelo Vanderbilt upon her marriage in 1895 to the duke of Marlborough: however, she disliked it, complaining in her memoirs, *The Glitter and the Gold* (1953), that it always gave her a headache, and soon after she separated from the duke she sold it at Christie's. May Goelet, married in 1903 to the duke of Roxburghe, made a great impression at the state opening of

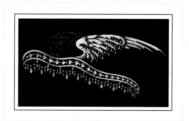

Chaumet design (c.1900) for
Valkyrie wing tiara of Princess
de Polignac.

CHAUMET

Parliament in the coronation year of George V: "Her all-round crown was gorgeous, great pear-shaped diamonds forming spikes round the head, and other stones, equally large set to swing under these points of light," according to *Queen* (1911).

Some had several tiaras to choose from. Alice Roosevelt Longworth remembered those of her friend, Beatrice Ogden Mills, who married Lord Granard in 1909: "I stayed with her once at the delightful house her parents had in Paris. She said to me one day in her 'Mayfair' accent, 'Do you want to come shopping with me this afternoon, Alice? Sweet (her father) has promised to buy me a tiara for little dinners!' A tiara for little dinners. I ask you. Heaven knows what she had for the big ones." Mrs. Ogden Mills had already given her at least two as wedding presents—one of them a wreath of oak leaves, the Granard family badge, the other a pinnacled design surmounted by huge pear-shaped diamonds. The taste for tiaras remained with Beatrice Granard, for she could never resist a new one, and went on buying them until the end of her life. Equally enthusiastic was Nancy Langhorne, wife of Viscount Astor, for whom Cartier made a tiara mounted with the Sancy diamond (fifty-four carats) formerly owned by kings and queens of France and England and now in the Louvre. Rosina Harrison, her maid, recalled in *Rose, My Life in Service* (1975): "Apart from the Sancy diamond and the pearls, the other special pieces of jewelry were the tiaras. Her ladyship had five. The most beautiful was the Astor heirloom, the second was an exotic peacock bandeau of diamonds and pearls, the third aquamarines and diamonds, the fourth she bought herself—it was of spiky diamonds, and the fifth was an imitation of the first. It was used by her for the less important occasions and she also lent it to her friends. All her most precious jewelry was expensive to wear because from the moment it left the bank until its return there was a special premium in operation. Not that she ever stopped to think about that. She loved wearing it and she often used it too much for my taste. She'd turn round to me and say, 'How do I look, Rose?' and I'd reply, 'Haven't you forgotten the kitchen stove, my lady?' earning myself the customary 'Shut up, Rose.'"

Consuelo Vanderbilt dressed for the coronation of Edward VII (1902).

PRESERVATION SOCIETY OF NEWPORT COUNTY

Nancy, wife of Viscount Astor, wearing her tiara set with the Sancy diamond to a state opening of Parliament in 1948.

THE ILLUSTRATED LONDON NEWS PICTURE LIBRARY

Other leading London hostesses during the Belle Epoque were Mrs. John Mackay, widow of the California "silver king"; Mrs. Adair, said to be the greatest landowner in Texas; and Mrs. Arthur Paget. Each relied on her jeweler to ensure she stood out from the crowd, but none more so than Mrs. Mackay, who was invited by Queen Alexandra to bring her collection—acquired from Boucheron of Paris—to Buckingham Palace. There were further Anglo-American marriages after World War I, for instance, that of Barbara Murray and the earl of Moray (1924), followed by Philippa Wendell and the earl of Galloway (1924), Thelma Hays Morgan and Viscount Furness (1926), and Raffaele Kennedy and the duke of Leinster (1932). The Brooklyn-born duchess relates in *So Brief a Dream* (1973) how she was presented at court after her marriage with a tiara given as a wedding present by Lady d'Abernon, her husband's aunt: "It is all big diamonds in a delicate filigree setting with one large emerald at the top for Leinster in Ireland, I like to think. I wore a Schiaparelli white satin dress with a long emerald green velvet train to pick up the emerald, my hair long, white kid gloves, an enormous green feather fan and, of course, the white plumes of Wales." By that time another generation of hostesses had emerged. Some, for instance Lady Cunard, née Maude Burke of San Francisco, had married Englishmen, but two of the most indefatigably dedicated to London society, Mrs. William Corey and Mrs. James Corrigan, were widows of steel tycoons. Again, much of their wealth was spent on jewelry.

The pattern of marriage between American fortunes and European blue blood was not confined to England and France. Some Americans married Italians, and when Mrs. Mackay's only daughter, Eva, became Princess Fernando da Colonna di Galatro (1885), she gave her the jewels befitting her position in Roman society: a diamond parure with tiara included and diamond fern leaves, also for the hair. Other American-Italian marriages followed: Elizabeth Field to Prince Salvatore Brancaccio (1870), Charlotte Skinner to Count Albert de Foresta (1891), Josephine Curtis to Prince Poggio Suasi Ruspoli (1894), Elsie Moore to Prince Marino Torlonia (1907), and Margaret Preston Draper to Prince Andrea Buoncompagni Ludovisi (1916). Two others, well known in the interwar period, were America's "Princess Royal," Jane Watson, Princess de San Faustino, and Countess Dentice di Frasso. Of those who married

Princess Grace and Prince Rainier
of Monaco on their wedding day
(1956).

UPI/CORBIS-BETTMAN

German and Austrian titles, the best known was Frances Huntington, wife of Prince Edmond Hatzfeldt. At the time of her marriage in 1889, her father, Collis P. Huntington, declared "the Prince, like other men in his position, has had an inordinate capacity for spending money and getting into debt and difficulty. I wish he had a cleaner record, but he is a bright man of many and varied talents and will doubtless make my daughter happy. The sum which the Princess receives as her dowry is no more or less than what she would have taken if she had married a Connecticut farmer." This settlement must have been very handsome, for the princess became one of a celebrated group of London hostesses.

Of those who married into the Austro-Hungarian nobility, the best known was Gladys Moore Vanderbilt, wife of Count Laszlo Szechenyi (1908). Her wedding present from her mother was a magnificent laurel tiara, the leaves meeting at a detachable pear-shaped diamond (62.05 carats) in the center. It was worn at all the court functions of Vienna and Budapest, and there is a photograph of her resplendent in lace and velvet at the coronation of the last Habsburg emperor, Charles IV (1916), though the diamond has been taken from the tiara and hangs as a pendant to her necklace. According to *Femina* (1906), no fewer than six great Russian grandees had married Americans, including Frances Whitehouse of New York, wife of Baron Ramsay, master of ceremonies at the imperial court of St. Petersburg. Even after the Russian Revolution of 1917 deprived the Russian husbands of their property and sent them into exile, they continued to attract American women of means. Alice Astor married Prince Serge Obolensky (1924), and Barbara Hutton, who married Prince Midvani (1933), commissioned from Chaumet and Cartier sets of jewelry on a truly royal scale. Further purchases of jewelry marked the latter's marriages to the Danish count Haugwitz Reventlow and the Russian prince Troubetzkoy: tiaras remained a passion until the end of her life. Two of the most remarkable were made after World War II. From Cartier she ordered a tiara/necklace combination of Indian style for a group of magnificent emeralds once owned by the grand duchess Vladimir (1947) and from Van Cleef & Arpels, a Mary Stuart design mounted with a superb collection of pear-shaped, marquise, and brilliant-cut diamonds (1967).

Only royalty seemed to remain aloof from the charms of the American girl with her personal attractions, easy manner, and large fortune. The exception was Prince Christopher of Greece, married to the widow Mrs. Nancy Leeds, who took the name of Princess Anastasia (1920). She could play the role to perfection, owning as she did three of Cartier's most celebrated tiaras. The first, which stood high on the head, was mounted with seven large pear-shaped diamonds, linked by Louis XVI–style festoons (1907); the second was a bandeau of interlaced diamond circles each enclosing an alternate diamond or pearl swinging within (1913) and the third, which she wears in her portrait by Philip de Laszlo, was an emerald-and-diamond halo, matching the huge stones in her necklace (1921).

Posted abroad as representatives of a democratic republic, few American diplomatic wives could resist completing their dress for court and official functions with a glittering tiara, even if borrowed

Gladys Moore Vanderbilt, wife
of Count Laszlo Szechenyi, at the
coronation of the last Habsburg
emperor, Charles IV, in 1916.

or hired for the occasion. At least three American ambassadors bought tiaras from Chaumet during the Belle Epoque: Henry White (Paris, 1906–09) bought a diamond-and-pearl floral design for his wife Daisy; Myron Herrick (Paris, 1912–14, 1921–29) bought a Mary Stuart–style halo filled in with leafy sprays; and George Sickles (Brussels, 1901) purchased a Louis XVI garland pattern with flowers tied with ribbons. Other Americans known for their tiaras were Mrs. Whitelaw Reid and her daughter, Jean, wife of the Hon. John Ward, whose hospitality at the London embassy was legendary; Lady Lowther, the former Alice Blight of Philadelphia; Cornelia van Rensseaeller Thayer, married to the Danish Count Charles von Moltke; and the actress Madeleine Bouton, wife of the Russian military attaché in Paris, Count Nostitz.

Inevitably, there were not so many in the interwar years, and when Rose, wife of Joseph Kennedy, was presented at court in 1938, she wore a tiara belonging to a friend, the Countess of Bessborough. She borrowed another, set with rubies and diamonds, for the state opening of Parliament (1939). The coronations of 1937 and 1953 encouraged the American women invited to dress up, and Mrs. Bingham, wife of the ambassador, appeared with one of the most imposing tiaras for the festivities when George VI and Queen Elizabeth were crowned (1937). In 1953, Mrs. Perle Mesta, U.S. ambassador to the duchy of Luxembourg, brought a tiara to wear at all the London parties, including her own, held at Claridge's. Before her arrival in London, where her husband had been appointed ambassador in 1957, Mrs. John Hay Whitney, recognizing the need for a tiara for the social life of that time, asked Fulco di Verdura to make her one. Inspired by the feathered headdress of Native Americans, his gold-and-diamond design struck a patriotic note, as well as suiting her dark looks. During the Whitneys' time at the embassy and before and after it, Douglas Fairbanks, Jr., worked so hard to further Anglo-American friendship that he was made an honorary knight (1950). That year, he was photographed with his wife; he with his decorations, she with her tiara.

Barbara Hutton's Mary Stuart diamond tiara, made by Van Cleef & Arpels (1967).

VAN CLEEF & ARPELS

Lady Lowther wearing a diamond tiara from Chaumet (1908).

THE ILLUSTRATED LONDON NEWS PICTURE LIBRARY

According to the French magazine *Femina* (1906), a group of public-spirited Americans, appalled by the drain of money away from its place of origin as a result of so many marriages with titled Europeans, had founded a League for the Prevention of Fortune Hunters. By this date, it was by no means necessary for those who wished to display wealth to have to frequent foreign courts and embassies, for in America itself colossal fortunes were being spent on erecting palaces and filling them with works of art, entertaining on a grand scale, and buying beautiful clothes and jewelry. Henry James, invited to dine in New York, described in *The American Scene* (1905): "The scene of our feast was a palace and the perfection of setting and service absolute: the ladies, beautiful, gracious and glittering with gems, were in tiaras and with a resemblance of court trains—a sort of predescribed official magnificence." The former Elizabeth Drexel, once married to the social clown Harry Lehr, also remembered in *King Lehr and the Gilded Age* (1935), "These were the days of magnificence, when money was poured out like water. Nothing but the best was good enough, and the best had to be procured regardless of cost. The new kings of trade might work at their offices 12, 14 hours a day but their wives would have something to show for it . . . evenings given over to balls, to dinner parties . . . evenings at the Opera where every woman wore full regalia to outshine her neighbours. Diamond tiaras, ropes of pearls, enormous sapphires, emeralds in such profusion that the problem was to find a novel way of wearing them."

Tiffany's had been making jeweled head ornaments, including tiaras, since the 1870s, and one of their best customers, Mrs. Leland Stanford, was painted in Paris by Leon Bonnat wearing a diamond tiara from that firm with her Worth gown. The acknowledged "queen of diamonds," Jane Stanford spent one million dollars on stones purchased from Queen Isabella of Spain, then living in exile in Paris. She also owned four parures of different-colored diamonds—violet, yellow, pink, and white, each completed by a tiara. As one of the chief buyers at the dispersal of the French crown jewels in Paris (1887),

The Hon. R. W. Bingham (U.S. Ambassador) and Mrs. Bingham dressed for the coronation of George VI in 1937.

THE ILLUSTRATED LONDON NEWS PICTURE LIBRARY

Mr. and Mrs. Douglas Fairbanks, Jr. (1950).

THE ILLUSTRATED LONDON NEWS PICTURE LIBRARY

Mrs. Leland Stanford, painted by
Léon Bonnat, wearing her Tiffany
tiara (1881).

Tiffany's purchased the ruby-and-diamond parure made by M. E. Nitot & Fils, predecessor of Chaumet, in 1810. This was on behalf of Mrs. Bradley Martin of New York, who gave it to her daughter, Cornelia, Countess Craven. The superb tiara is now in the Niarchos collection. Another Tiffany customer was Mrs. William Astor, who led New York society from her mansion on Fifth Avenue: "She was really homely, no looks at all," remembered one of her nieces, "yet dressed in her Worth gown, weighed down with her jewels, a diamond tiara in her dyed black hair, she appeared more regal ruling over her 400 [the maximum number her ballroom could hold] than Queen Victoria ruling over the British Empire." Escorted by ten mounted policemen, she capitulated to her rival, Mrs. Alva Vanderbilt, by attending the costume ball held at the latter's new family mansion dressed as a Venetian princess with her tiara of diamond stars and jewelry worth eight hundred thousand dollars. She wore this tiara, with full evening dress and large stomacher brooch, to Harry Lehr's dinners at Sherry's restaurant on Sunday evenings. Others did likewise dining at restaurants, or in private homes, at Newport balls or sitting in the diamond horseshoe of the Metropolitan Opera House.

Just as in the early nineteenth century the marchioness of Londonderry dazzled with the jewels she took on her travels, so now did the American women on their visits to Europe. There was Mrs. John Drexel, whose diamonds caused a sensation at the courts of Berlin and Dresden, and Grace Wilson, who married Cornelius Vanderbilt II (1896). Embarking from their yacht, the *North Star*, for a visit to the opera in Rome, she related: "I hear that all the Italian papers speak of me and my jewels. I wore my tiara, my emerald collar, my pearls with the emerald piece . . . my diamond fringe across the front of my gown (they admire that extravagantly) and my other emerald piece—all this with my yellow and silver gown looked very pretty." Later in life she preferred to place her tiara over a bandeau matching her dress, even when attending the opera, where she boasted that the conductor bowed to her for permission to start the overture. During the Gilded Age, all her Vanderbilt relations were buying from Cartier, which established a New York branch in 1909. One of the best customers was Gertrude Vanderbilt, whose marriage in 1896

Mrs. John R. Drexel in Berlin court
gown and jewels (c. 1911).

to Harry Payne Whitney, heir to the Standard Oil fortune, was immensely popular: to mark the general satisfaction that she had found a husband at home and not abroad, the band played the "Star Spangled Banner" at their wedding. Her father gave her a tiara then, and on her own account she bought others such as a pair of Valkyrie wings from Chaumet (1910) and was photographed by Baron de Meyer for *Vogue*, resplendent in a diamond *kokoshnik*. Other New Yorkers who bought tiaras from Chaumet were Mrs. Perry Belmont (a waterfall design diamond tiara, and pearl-and-diamond tiara, 1899) and Mrs. Cass Canfield (a ribbon and bowknot design with pear-shaped diamonds, 1894). Subsequently, as Mrs. F. Gray Griswold, she bought another (a Greek-key pattern with ribbon design, 1907). J. P. Morgan bought the first diamond triple-sun tiara from Cartier (1904), and this firm was given the task of mounting five fabulous emerald and diamond peacock feathers into a tiara for Mrs. George Gould, well known for her magnificent pearls. Chaumet tiaras went to residents of other cities, too: Mr. Thayer (1899), Mrs. Henry Sears, and Mr. Ames (both 1904) of Boston, Mr. Crawford Hill (1905 and 1907) of Denver, and Mr. MacClean (1911) of Washington. Cartier clients in Philadelphia were overshadowed by Mrs. Eva Stotesbury, who married "Morgan's man" in that city (1912). Given three tiaras as wedding presents, she wore one of them for her first appearance at the Philadelphia Opera: "Her majestic figure swathed in a dress of white satin with a net of silver and crystal spangles. Over this she threw a long purple cloak with heavy swags of fox fur at the collar and cuffs. On her bosom lay the Stotesbury pearls looped in four coils, and above these at the throat were the Morgan diamonds (her wedding present from J. P. Morgan). But the climax of her costume was the diamond tiara, the most beautiful ever seen at the Metropolitan Opera House and at the Academy of Music" (Stephen Birmingham, *The Grandes Dames*, 1982). In Washington Mrs. Evelyn Walsh MacClean caused similar amazement with the "Star of the East" (92½ carat) diamond in the aigrette on her head, and the blue Hope Diamond hanging from the pearls at her neck, both from Cartier (1908, 1910).

Although the Gilded Age came to an end with World War I, the tiara survived the great political and social changes that followed, though its role was greatly diminished. Grace Vanderbilt kept the flag flying when she spent three hundred thousand dollars on a diamond bandeau for her daughter-in-law, Rachel (1920), for she said "no Vanderbilt wife could do without one." Mrs. Stotesbury indulged in yet another tiara from Cartier (1923): the weight of the emeralds and diamonds was too much—it listed across her head and fell over her ear, and gave her a stiff neck. Yet, a new generation was discovering the tiara, amusingly alluded to by Anita Loos in *Gentleman Prefer Blondes* (1925), whose protagonist, Lorelei Lee, was impressed by one for sale in London: "I think a diamond tiara is delightful because it is a place where I really never thought of wearing diamonds before and I thought I had almost one of everything until I saw a diamond tiara . . . I have set my heart on a diamond tiara."

The stock market crash of 1929, with its trail of bankruptcies and suicides, brought all displays of luxury to a temporary halt. Recovery was on the way by the mid 1930s when bankers' wives, such as Mrs. Boyce Thompson, were ordering new tiaras from Chaumet, and when the audience at the Metropolitan Opera House brought their jewels out again for opening night. However, for the period after World War II, it is significant that the Austrian jeweler Marianne Ostier, who had designed the picturesque tiara of Queen Geraldine of Albania (1938), moved to New York, where as well as making jewels, she wrote a book, *Jewels and the Woman* (1958), in which she observed that "few women outside of the nobility on state occasions wear the metal bands set or peaked with gems, indiscriminately called diadems or tiaras." The tradition in America was, with few exceptions, maintained by the grandes dames of Washington and of Palm Beach, who for decades brought out their tiaras whenever they entertained royalty and often when royalty was not present. Two of the most prominent, whose reigns extended well into the 1960s, were Mrs. Robert Woods Bliss (1879–1969) and Mrs. Marjorie Merriweather Post (1887–1973). From her youth, as the wife of a diplomat, Mrs. Bliss was accustomed to wearing tiaras, several of them bought from Chaumet. Mrs. Post, who, as a philanthropist and wife of a man in public service, was very much in the public eye throughout her long life, had a collection of tiaras from different periods. The earliest was originally made for the Empress Marie Louise, with the emeralds replaced by turquoises, worn with an important turquoise necklace and earrings. She could alternate this classical design with a "traditional romantic" garland of flowers or the contemporary chic of an all-white Art Deco tiara. Today, although few women are prepared to become national institutions in the mold of Mrs. Bliss and Mrs. Post, there are still many who own tiaras that they keep for occasions of particular brilliance and elegance.

THE ARTISTIC TIARA

At the time of the Paris International Exhibition (1900), the jewelry world was divided. On the one hand, there were the great exponents of the garland style, led by Boucheron, Cartier, Chaumet, and Mellerio, who regarded their task as that of showing off valuable stones to their best advantage, preferably in

Mrs. Marjorie Merriweather Post at the Red Cross Ball in 1967, wearing the tiara made for the Empress Marie Louise, turquoise necklace, and earrings.

DAVIDOFF STUDIOS, PALM BEACH

Mrs. Robert Woods Bliss (1908).

HARVARD UNIVERSITY ARCHIVES

designs evoking the arts of eighteenth-century France. In contrast, the second group, led by René Lalique (1860–1945), was determined to transform the appearance of jewelry by introducing new themes independent of the past and by using new materials—molded glass, ivory, horn—and *plique à jour* enamels applied to cells like stained glass. Those belonging to this Art Nouveau school thought that the beauty of a jewel lay in the perfection of the artistic conception and not in the precious stones used: they believed that the value of the materials was of secondary importance to their appropriateness in the design. The designs, influenced by Japanese art, were almost always derived from nature—butterflies, dragonflies, moths, sweet peas, thistle, cyclamen, and nymphs with beautiful faces and long flowing locks. Although most Art Nouveau head ornaments are combs with decorated tops, some of these poet jewelers did propose alternatives to the glittering diamond tiara so typical of Belle Epoque taste. Baron Robert de Rothschild bought a tiara considered to be the masterpiece of René Lalique as a wedding present for Nelly Beer (1907), and there is another by the same artist in the Musée des Arts Décoratifs, Paris, acquired by the art-loving Countess de Béhague. It is a sculptural design of a mermaid, twin tails coiled around two opals. High above her head she brandishes a third opal, flashing out light and colors that contrast with the patinated bronze figure. More typical and easier to wear are the naturalistic tiaras—a branch of hazelnuts, a spray of apple blossom, two grasshoppers face-to-face—executed by Lalique and his followers such as Georges Fouquet, Eugène Feuillâtre, Henri Vever, and Louis Aucoc. However, these creations were not cheap, and *Femina* (1909) condemned Art Nouveau ornaments for failing to meet the first requirement of all jewelry; namely, to go with everything. Notwithstanding its success in artistic circles, Art Nouveau was a spent force by 1914, since wealthy female customers remained faithful to conventional jewelers and to the idea of investing in precious stones.

Across the English Channel there was a parallel development called the Arts and Crafts movement, which turned to an ideal of craftsmanship and artistic design, similarly independent of intrinsic value. The jewelry of these followers of William Morris and John Ruskin is very different from Art Nouveau: the ornament is always symmetrical, the floral motifs are rigid, and it was executed for people of modest means rather than for rich aesthetes. The dominant figures were Henry Wilson (1864–1942), his colleague John Paul Cooper (1869–1933), and C. R. Ashbee (1863–1942), founder, in 1888, of the Guild of Handicraft. Also in 1888, the well-known firm Liberty and Co. opened a jewelry department selling Celtic-style jewels by Archibald Knox and Jessie King and tiaras made of horn and set with moonstones by Frederick James Partridge (1877–1942). Others made them, too, for as a quintessentially English jewel there was a continuous demand for the Arts and Crafts version of the tiara. Unlike the Art Nouveau, the British Arts and Crafts movement survived the difficult years of World War I, and after World War II emerged again, much encouraged by Graham Hughes, artistic director of the Company of Goldsmiths.

Butterfly coronet (c.1900), by
Eugène Feuillâtre.

CHAPTER 1 THE AGE OF NAPOLEON

The nine nicolo intaglios, which are graduated in size from the center to the back, are framed in double borders of milled gold, encircled by a row of pearls with pearl clusters between. The intaglios represent, from the left to right, Cupid burning Psyche in the guise of a butterfly; Omphale carrying the club of Hercules; Bonus Eventus holding a cornucopia; Cupid with his bow and arrow; Hercules facing right in profile, after the ancient gem signed GNAIOS; Portrait of a man, perhaps Pompey; Venus undressing for the bath; Cupid testing the sharpness of his arrow; and Cupid whipping Psyche in the guise of a butterfly. Family tradition associates this tiara, which was formerly in the collection of the Duke of Bedford, with Caroline Murat, Queen of Naples. She sold it to the sixth duke, through the agency of a mutual friend, the Comte de Flahaut, former *aide de camp* to Joachim Murat. The design and workmanship compare with the cameo tiara attributed to Nitot & Fils, now in the collection of the king of Sweden, inherited from the Empress Josephine.

MIKIMOTO

French fashion plate (1804) showing a bandeau set with intaglios worn low on the forehead with hair dressed in a revival of classical style.

MUSEUM OF FINE ARTS, BOSTON.

BANDEAU C. 1810 NITOT & FILS(?), FRENCH
Gold, pearls, nicolo intaglios.

The empress, attired in a white and silver dress, stands beside the imperial crown and wears a parure of diamonds comprising tiara, comb, girandole (three-drop) earrings, necklace, and belt made by Nitot & Fils in 1811, court jewelers to Napoleon, and founders of the Parisian house of Chaumet. The most magnificent stones—the Fleur de Pecher, the Mazarin VIII, the Grand Mazarin, and the diamond of the king of Sardinia—were mounted in the center palmette, side honeysuckles, and scrolls of the tiara, which epitomizes the classical style of the First Empire. With the exception of the necklace, all these jewels were returned to the treasury after Napoleon's defeat at Waterloo and were eventually dispersed when the French crown jewels were sold by the Third Republic in 1887. The necklace, which Napoleon had given the Empress Marie Louise upon the birth of their son, the king of Rome in 1811, is now in the Smithsonian Institution.

CHAUMET, PARIS

The original parure was made for Empress Marie Louise by Nitot & Fils in 1811. The rubies and diamonds were later removed and made into jewels for the Duchesse d'Angoulême, and then dispersed at the sale of the French crown jewels in 1887. This replica was created by Chaumet (c. 1900) from the original design in homage to its founders, Nitot & Fils.

CHAUMET, PARIS

PORTRAIT OF EMPRESS MARIE LOUISE 1812 ROBERT LEFÈVRE
Oil on canvas

• •

The jet is faceted into beads, polished to gleam brightly, and mounted on a base of gilt bronze. The beads are massed together into a wide circlet, which is surmounted by a sequence of jet pear-shaped drops supported by scrolls alternating with rosettes. Another queen who wore a jet coronet like this was Louise of Prussia, whose beauty impressed the artist Madame Vigée Le Brun (1801): "She was in deep mourning and wore a coronet of black jet, which far from being to her disadvantage, brought out the dazzling whiteness of her skin." Made in different heights, both high and low, and in various designs, those derived from heraldry had a regal and aristocratic character. *Queen* (1867) reported: "Jet diadems remain very much in favor and the aristocracy have chosen a very original idea of giving them an individual value. They order their heraldic coronets to be decorated with large round beads like the coronet of a countess, others with fleurons like that of a marchioness. I saw the other day two noble belles, the Countess de Lutrat and the Duchess de Frias, each wearing a black lace bonnet with their respective coronets in jet." This coronet, which was part of the mourning parure of Hortense (1783–1837), daughter of the Empress Josephine and married to Louis Bonaparte, king of Holland, was a gift to her lady-in-waiting, Valerie Mazuyer, who was also goddaughter of the empress.

MUSÉE NATIONAL DE MALMAISON

QUEEN HORTENSE'S CORONET c. 1810 FRENCH
Jet, gilt bronze.

• •
61

The tiara, from a suite with a matching necklace and top and drop earrings, is designed around the classical motifs of vine leaves, interspersed with medallions with milled gold rims enclosing copies of well-known cameos. In the tiara, these represent the Labors of Hercules, Ganymede, and Methe with her wine cup. Jewelry of this type was produced in the iron foundries of Berlin from 1804, and demand for it was so great that eventually there were forty-seven firms supplying it. A high point was reached in 1813 when, during the War of Liberation from Napoleon's armies, German women exchanged their gold jewelry, particularly rings, for Berlin iron ornaments. Some such are inscribed with a patriotic slogan in German, translating as "I gave gold for iron." As an alternative to jet, iron was adopted internationally to wear with mourning dress. The beautiful wife of the impecunious civil servant, M. Rabourdin, in Balzac's novel *Les Employés* (1824), dresses in black with Berlin iron and jet jewelry when invited to a reception by the minister of her husband's department. She was the best-dressed woman there, for her black dress emphasized her slim figure, and the vine leaves in the tiara mingled charmingly with her hair, as if on a branch. Contemporary fashion plates show that black jewelry was not worn exclusively by those in mourning, but also with clothes of bright color, especially pink.

ALBION ART, JAPAN

MOURNING TIARA c. 1810 GERMAN
Iron, gold.

• •

The tiara is composed of an open-work band of pairs of diamonds set alternatively above and below between button pearls, except in the center, which is marked by a diamond between three small pearls. The seven pear pearls in diamond caps rise from addorsed diamond scrolls linked together like festoons, each pair enclosing a collet-set diamond. This grand court jewel from a German princely family could be worn above the brow or over the chignon at the back of the head, in the manner introduced by Queen Marie de Médicis at the beginning of the seventeenth century, and adopted by her daughter Queen Henrietta Maria of England and the ladies of her court. Queen Victoria wears a diamond and sapphire tiara in this way in a portrait by F. X. Winterhalter (1842), now in Windsor Castle.

S. J. PHILLIPS LTD., LONDON

Thomas Couture sketch for a portrait (1856) of Princess Mathilde Bonaparte wearing two tiaras, one in the front of the head, the other at the back, over the chignon, Marie de Médicis style.

MUSÉE NATIONAL DU CHATEAU DE COMPIEGNE

FESTOON TIARA   C. 1830   GERMAN
Gold, silver, button and pear pearls, diamonds.

The open-work tiara is part of a parure with matching top and drop earrings, belt clasp, and necklace with drop-shaped pendant. The full beauty of the stones is revealed by this simple design and unobtrusive setting. The parure could have been that which *The Mirror of Fashion* (1829) reported after a ball at Ranelagh, "where many ladies were splendidly dressed: one young lady wore on her hair a superb ornament of topazes with earrings, necklace and bracelets of the same golden colored gems, which were of the rarest and most valuable kind." It was the fashion of the time to place the tiara rather low on the brow, with ringlets to each side, and the hair piled up behind held in place by a comb with floral bouquets placed to the side.

TOPAZ TIARA 1820s ENGLISH (?)
Gold, golden topazes.

• •

Two sprays of mixed flowers, entirely pavéd with diamonds, meet at the large, open wild rose in the center. The sprays can also be worn as brooches. The diamonds, set in flowers, are recorded in the Heathcote inventory of 1786 and have descended in the same family since. The court jewelers, Rundell, Bridge, and Rundell, who enjoyed international fame, supplied jewelry of this quality to George IV, and to other customers such as the art-loving George Watson Taylor. Shortly after inheriting a fortune in 1815, Taylor bought from Rundell's a "brilliant ornament for the headdress consisting of a handsome sprig with large flowers" and "a very magnificent Brilliant wreath composed of the flowers and leaves of the Hydrangea."

BARONESS WILLOUGHBY DE ERESBY

The countess of Ancaster in her coronation robes, tiara on her head, and the floral sprays pinned to her bodice. The diamond chain shown below the photograph formed the base of the tiara crowning her head (1902).

THE GRIMSTHORPE AND DRUMMOND CASTLE TRUSTEES

HEATHCOTE TIARA　c. 1800 and later　ENGLISH
Gold, silver, diamonds.

• •

The pavéd diamond leaves are earlier in date than the daisies in this tiara, which could be a replacement for the original family tiara of the earls of Rosebery. This was described as one of the presents given by the fifth earl of Rosebery upon his marriage to Hannah Rothschild in 1878: "The Rosebery family jewel, a wreath of jasmine and leaves," displayed at the reception, "surrounded by thousands of scented roses." Presumably, the jasmine flowers were later removed and the popular daisies put in their place. A garland of jasmine flowers would have exemplified fashionable taste for naturalistic floral jewelry, especially for the head, in the Romantic period, pioneered by Fossin/Chaumet of Paris. The tiara is known by the name of the Rosebery family, Primrose, and, as an heirloom, is usually worn by daughters and daughters-in-law at weddings.

THE EARL AND COUNTESS OF ROSEBERY

The long spray of flowers, leaves and buds curves round into a half circle, surmounted in the front by crossed leafy stems with a flower head between, and two others to the sides, detachable for use as a brooch and earrings. Exemplifying the English ancestral jewel, this tiara, like the Heathcote (p. 69) and Primrose tiaras, has been in the same family since it was made, and because of the national taste for naturalistic motifs has never been out of fashion.

THE TRUSTEES OF THE RT. HON. OLIVE, COUNTESS FITZWILLIAM'S CHATTELS SETTLEMENT, BY PERMISSION OF LADY JULIET TADGELL

↑ PRIMROSE TIARA C. 1830 and later ENGLISH
Gold, silver, diamonds.

↓ FITZWILLIAM TIARA C. 1820 ENGLISH
Gold, silver, diamonds.

The tiara consists of three bouquets of leaves, flowers, and ears of wheat wrought in gold and set with semiprecious and hard stones of colors chosen for their naturalistic effect. It was designed to be worn at summer parties when diamonds were customarily put away until the winter. Perhaps combined with bunches of artificial flowers, these bouquets grouped together would seem to have been freshly picked from the garden.

MUSEUM OF LONDON

An English fashion plate (1823) of a young woman in evening dress with jewelry—bracelet, necklace, earrings, and a wreath of gold leaves placed well above the brow. This type of tiara of metal, sometimes enamelled, has never gone out of fashion. The actress Jamie Lee Curtis had one on her head at the state opening of Parliament in November 1998, when she accompanied her husband, Lord Haden Guest.

MUSEUM OF FINE ARTS, BOSTON

SUMMER TIARA C. 1835 ENGLISH
Gold, carnelians, amethysts, garnets, aquamarines, peridots, chrysoprases, citrines, turquoises, pearls.

The branches of coral, graduated toward the back of the head, meet in the center, above the brow, like a wreath. Other tiaras mounted with coral cameos and framed in gold and pearls were worn during the First Empire by both the Empress Josephine and Empress Marie Louise; from Naples, Queen Caroline, Napoleon's sister sent the best specimens. Although most women preferred coral in beads or cameos, there were a few who wore the natural branches like this standing up on the head and encircling the neck. The noble red color was thought to look best with white ball dresses. This tiara and its matching brooch, which belonged to Queen Mary, wife of George V, most likely belonged to her mother, Princess Mary of Cambridge (1833–97).

MUSEUM OF LONDON

In this hand-colored print (1830), the figure on the right is wearing a suite of coral jewelry in branches: necklace, earrings, wreath above the brow, comb at the back of the head, and brooch pinned to the sash above the hem of her white ball dress.

PRIVATE COLLECTION

TIARA c. 1840 NEAPOLITAN
Coral, gilt metal.

The tiara rests on a base of alternate round pearls and diamond leaves, surmounted by seven vertical elements between eight cartouches. Each vertical element consists of a round pearl below two pear pearls, with a crescent supporting the upper pearl. Similarly, there is a pear pearl at the top of each cartouche so that the head is crowned by a magnificent undulating line. Appointed court jeweler by Napoleon III in 1853, Gabriel Lemonnier (1808–1884) used pearls in the state treasury since the reign of Henri IV and Marie de Medicis, and others acquired by Napoleon for the splendid pearl parures of the Empresses Josephine and Marie Louise. Part of a set consisting of coronet, brooches, necklaces, and bracelets worn by the Empress Eugénie, it was sold with the French crown jewels by the Third Republic (1887) and thereafter acquired by Prince Albert Thurn and Taxis on his marriage to the Archduchess Marguerite, great granddaughter of Louis Philippe (1890). It remained in that family until 1991 when the *Société des Amis du Louvre* bought it for the Galerie d'Apollon (Sotheby's Geneva, November 1992). George Kunz, author of *The Book of the Pearl* (1908), was impressed by the pearl jewelry of the Empress Eugénie and admired this tiara most of all for "the exceptionally artistic openwork design." The empress wears it above the brow, with the matching coronet behind, no less than eight rows of pearls at her neck, and a white dress for the portrait by F. X. Winterhalter (1855), and again in a marble bust by Georges Diébolt.

MUSÉE DU LOUVRE, DÉPARTEMENT DES OBJETS D'ART

THE EMPRESS EUGÉNIE'S TIARA 1853 GABRIEL LEMONNIER, FRENCH
Gold, silver, pearls, diamonds.

• • •

The continuous line of large brilliants curved to the back of the head is surmounted by swags linking a succession of palm motifs, centers mounted on trembler springs, all richly pavéd with 1,141 brilliant cut diamonds, weighing 482½ carats. It was part of the parure made in the opulent grand Victorian court style by the crown jeweler Garrard for the Marchioness of Londonderry (1800–62) using the family collection of Golconda and Brazilian diamonds. Just as her dazzling appearance inspired the descriptions of the bejeweled heroines in the novels of Benjamin Disraeli, so, too, have the wives of her descendants worn this tiara to similar great effect. According to the *Illustrated London News* (1911), the reigning marchioness was a wonderful sight as she walked to her place in Westminster Abbey for the coronation of George V: "Literally the size of small pears, the celebrated Londonderry pearls are unique, each point of her deep coronet of brilliants being finished off with these superb stones." Again, after the state opening of Parliament in 1924, the same magazine approved the Londonderry jewels as "a heritage, and one in which Britishers all round take a vicarious pride."

THE LONDONDERRY FAMILY

Lafayette photograph of the marchioness of Londonderry with her daughters (1927).

NATIONAL PORTRAIT GALLERY, LONDON

LONDONDERRY TIARA 1854 R.S. GARRARD & CO., ENGLISH
Gold, silver, diamonds.

SCROLLWORK TIARA C. 1880 ENGLISH
Gold, silver, diamonds, pear-shaped pearls.
See page 84

PANSY TIARA   c. 1860   FRENCH (?)
Gold, silver, diamonds.
See page 84

•••

FLORAL TIARA C. 1860 MELLERIO DITS MELLER, FRENCH
Gold, silver, turquoises, diamonds.
See page 85

MARRIAGE TIARA AND BROOCH 1850 MAPPIN AND WEBB, ENGLISH
Silver.

See page 85

• •

The band of collet-set diamonds in pairs between smaller stones is graduated toward the back and crowned by open scrolls above clusters surmounted by pear pearls in diamond caps, with fleurs-de-lis between. The large pearl in the center, which forms the climax of this light and elegant design, was a gift from the Grand Duchess Vladimir, wife of the uncle of Tsar Nicholas II, to the Princess Galitzine, who wore it on a diamond ribbon brooch.

PRIVATE COLLECTION

The tiara consists of three pansy flowers in full bloom with leaves between all pavéd with diamonds. Mounted on a frame to wear on the head, it is divisible into three brooches. Recalling his childhood during the French Second Empire, the writer André Beaunier, in *Visages de France* (1913), recalled how at night the women with their diamond jewelry seemed to have chandeliers and gardens on their heads, and this tiara might have been one of the jewels he spoke of. The pansy is decorative in itself, but it has additional significance; since the name in French, *pensée*, means "think of me," the pansy was therefore widely used in jewelry, though rarely as a tiara.

THE HON. MRS. JOHN HASTINGS BASS

The tiara, mounted on a frame, consists of a continuous trail of flowers, leaves, and buds with turquoise centers and diamond petals. Clearly imitated from nature, the flowers have an organic quality and would seem freshly picked from the garden when placed in the hair.

MELLERIO DITS MELLER, PARIS

Both the wreath for the head and the brooch are made of silver myrtle leaves, sacred to Venus, and being evergreen, symbolic of faithful love. Because of these associations, myrtle was widely adopted for the bridal crown at weddings. This suite had a special significance for the family for whom it was first made, since the lid of the case is inscribed with the names and dates of three generations of brides who wore it on their wedding days: the first in 1853 and the last, during World War II, in 1940. For the marriage of Emily Bootle Wilbraham with the earl of Crawford and Balcarres (1869), Castellani made his version of a myrtle tiara, executed in gold and pearls: it is now in the Victoria and Albert Museum in London. Another interesting tiara in the same spirit was given by the marquess of Bute to his wife on the birth of their child (1876): it bore a ruby inscription in Hebrew letters that translates as "A virtuous woman is a crown to her husband."

TADEMA GALLERY, LONDON

The tiara consists of fourteen sections, each with two berries and three pavé-set laurel leaves, graduated toward the central five-petaled flower, with stamens framing a large square-shaped stone. It can be divided into smaller ornaments. As jewelers to the Empress Eugénie and Isabella II of Spain, Mellerio had mastered the court style of the Second Empire, one of the outstanding periods in the history of Parisian jewelry. When exhibited at the Paris International Exhibition (1867), the tiara was admired by the art critic Jules Mesnard for its pure and severe classicism and for so successfully combining a rich effect with good taste. It was bought by Victor Emmanuel II of Italy for his daughter-in-law, Margherita of Genoa Savoy, who married the future Umberto I in 1868. The laurel motif could reflect the influence of the classical jewelry in the Campana Collection displayed in the Louvre, and evoking the glory of imperial Rome was particularly appropriate for a queen of Italy whose capital was that city.

ALBION ART, JAPAN

Queen Margherita of Italy (1908) wearing her pearl and diamond fender with the pearl necklaces presented to her on each wedding anniversary by her husband, Umberto I, who had a passion for pearls.

PRIVATE COLLECTION

Queen Margherita of Italy wearing her celebrated pearl necklaces, pearl earrings, and the laurel tiara made by Mellerio in 1867.

CHRISTIE'S

QUEEN MARGHERITA'S LAUREL TIARA   1867   MELLERIO DITS MELLER, FRENCH
Gold, silver, diamonds.

The tall tiara, which surmounts a band interspersed with stones set square and lozenge-wise, consists of a graduated sequence of crescents enclosing large collet stones flanked by leafy scrolls with stylized lilies rising above them, and smaller lilies between. Described by the *Illustrated London News* (1878) as a "lustrous court diadem with some unusually large stones," it was a present from the earl of Rosebery to the heiress Hannah Rothschild upon their marriage. As the wife of an important statesman and a leading figure in London society, she would have been invited to many grand occasions when a tiara of this height and opulence—called a fender—would have been appropriate.

THE EARL AND COUNTESS OF ROSEBERY

The tiara rests on a band of pairs of stylized buds between collet-set diamonds, surmounted by a sequence of palmettes outlined by diamond borders linked at the base to lotus flowers graduated toward the back. The design is very close to that made in 1892 by Skinner of Orchard Street for the duchess of Devonshire, mother of the countess of Derby, who was presumably given this tiara at the time of her marriage in 1889. The imposing size and the severity of the classical motifs lend a majestic air to the tiara, entirely appropriate for the wife of a man whose wealth won him the title of "king of Lancashire." Their lives were spent in the center of the worlds of politics, racing, and diplomacy. With her "grand dame" presence, tact, and *savoir vivre* and his "grand seigneur" affability, their term at the embassy in Paris was the most fabulous in its long history. When they left in 1920, they were given a superlative send-off at the Gare du Nord. Since then the tiara has descended through three generations.

THE RIGHT HON. THE EARL OF DERBY

The Countess of Rosebery, née Hannah de Rothschild, at the time of her marriage.

PRIVATE COLLECTION

The Derby tiara worn upright like a crown by the countess of Derby at her wedding in October 1995.

THE RIGHT HON. THE EARL OF DERBY

↑ ROSEBERY TIARA 1878 FRENCH (?) ↓ DERBY TIARA C. 1890 SKINNER & CO.(?), ENGLISH
Gold, silver, diamonds. Gold, silver, diamonds.

From the engrailed pavéd diamond circlet rise five five-pointed stars similarly pavéd and centered on a button pearl within a raised border. Made famous by the Empress Elizabeth of Austria, who was painted by F. X. Winterhalter (1865) wearing stars in her hair pinned to a black velvet bandeau, stars sparkling with diamonds have been favored by women ever since. These were given by the daughter of Queen Victoria, Princess Louise, duchess of Argyll to her god-daughter and niece, Princess Victoria of Hesse, and the marchioness of Milford Haven, married to the First Sea Lord Prince Louis of Battenberg. She was on a visit to her sister, the Tsarina Alexandra Feodorovna in 1914 when war was declared and she had to leave for home in a great hurry. Since the jewels would have been a responsibility, the Tsarina suggested they should be left behind in her care. As is well known, the revolution of 1917 led to the disappearance of many valuables in Russia, including the Battenberg jewels, which were never seen again. Princess Louise therefore gave Princess Victoria this tiara to replace what had been lost. It then descended to her daughter-in-law, Edwina, future Countess Mountbatten of Burma, who had the stars remounted in a more modern style in the mid-1930s. She in turn gave the tiara to her daughter Patricia, the present Countess Mountbatten of Burma, as a wedding present upon her marriage to Lord Brabourne in 1946. She wore it to the court ball held at Buckingham Palace to celebrate the marriage of the future Queen Elizabeth II with the duke of Edinburgh in 1947, and it has been worn by her daughters and daughters-in-law at their weddings.

PRIVATE COLLECTION

Cecil Beaton (1937) photograph of the future Countess Mountbatten of Burma, wearing the star tiara for a *Vogue* magazine article on society women at the time of George VI's coronation.

THE BRITISH LIBRARY

STAR TIARA c. 1870, remounted 1937, ENGLISH
Gold, silver, diamonds, button pearls.

The pavéd diamond owl, wings stretched out wide, ruby and sapphire collar at the neck, crowned with ducal coronet, stands on a branch, firmly gripped by his claws, supported by the tiara frame. The Barons Middleton, who are descended from the Willoughby family, bear that name, and their wives wear the badge either on the head or as a stomacher brooch. It is one of the successes of English heraldic jewelry on account of its excellent quality and whimsical character.

PRIVATE COLLECTION

The tiara consists of a trail of graduated pavéd diamond ivy leaves and berries, mounted on a frame. As the badge of the Gordon family of Scotland, it was made for Miss Eliza Gordon Cumming upon her marriage to the future Lord Middleton in 1869: the bridegroom's father, the eighth Lord Middleton, paid eight hundred pounds for it, according to the ledgers of R. G. Hennell. The leaves are detachable for use as brooches, and they can be worn round the neck.

PRIVATE COLLECTION

Lady Middleton in court dress with veil, wearing both the Willoughby owl and the Gordon ivy tiara, c. 1875.

PRIVATE COLLECTION

The present Lady Middleton wearing the Gordon ivy tiara high on her head with a lace evening dress, c. 1960.

PRIVATE COLLECTION

↑ THE WILLOUGHBY OWL 1860s ENGLISH
Gold, silver, diamonds, rubies, sapphires.

↓ GORDON IVY TIARA 1869 R.G. HENNELL, ENGLISH
Gold, silver, diamonds.

• • •

The tiara consists of a branch of graduated oak leaves, pavé set, with the pearl acorns in diamond caps. Several old English families—the Howards, the Howard de Waldens, the Crichton Stuarts—own oak leaf tiaras, for it is their family badge. The oak leaf also has a patriotic significance and was adopted for jewelry celebrating the defeat of Napoleon by the British army and navy. The first owner of this example was given it for Christmas by her father, Albert Brassey, son of the great builder of the British railways, Thomas Brassey. Since she was very attached to a tiara that she already possessed, she never wore this one on her head, but divided it up into brooches.

PRIVATE COLLECTION, UNITED KINGDOM

The tiara consists of a trail of five graduated pavéd diamond wild dog roses with pairs of collet-set stones between, detachable for use as brooches. It illustrates the high Victorian taste for "Watteausesque" floral designs evocative of gracious eighteenth-century living. As the favorite flower of all ages, the rose has a place in English jewelry acquired by no other flower.

COLLECTION OF JOHN YORKE

The daughters of Albert Brassey, all bejeweled, with the oak spray worn as brooches by the daughter on the right.

PRIVATE COLLECTION

↑ OAK LEAF TIARA C. 1880 R.S. GARRARD
Gold, silver, pearls, diamonds.

↓ WILD ROSE TIARA C. 1880 ENGLISH
Gold, silver, diamonds.

The base, formed of a continuous line of diamonds, is surmounted by seven graduated turquoise and diamond open-work medallions alternating with drop-shaped clusters, linked by diamond ribbons interlacing beneath the drops. They are from the collection acquired for Charlotte Anne, who married the fifth duke of Buccleuch (1829) at a time when turquoises set either with diamonds or pearls were high fashion. Good specimens were difficult to find, and Queen Victoria asked Lady Stuart de Rothesay, the wife of her ambassador in St. Petersburg, to collect sufficient stones for a parure, which was made to the specifications of Prince Albert in "excellent taste," according to her journal (1843).

Photograph by Paul Shillabeer of Lady Caroline Montague Douglas Scott (1949) dressed as her ancestor, Mary Stuart, for an "auld alliance" (between France and Scotland) ball in Edinburgh. She wears family heirlooms and the turquoise and diamond tiara.

BUCCLEUCH TIARA c. 1850 ENGLISH
Gold, silver, turquoises, diamonds.

The open-work circlet curved to the head is enameled with pairs of stylized flower heads alternating with diamonds (now missing) and surmounted by medallions set with seven multilayered cameos standing out in relief between seven pairs of small monochrome intaglios, all on scrolled bases. The medallions are enameled black with translucent green-and-blue flower heads, outlined in white in the Holbein revival style and enriched with diamonds. The frames of the intaglios are enameled in various colors, some striped white. The gems, which were acquired by the second duke of Devonshire (1672–1729) include masterpieces by Graeco-Roman artists such as the sardonyx cameo of Aurora in her chariot, which is in the center, and two Tudor court portraits–Henry VIII and his children and Queen Elizabeth. The tiara is one of seven matching ornaments—comb, coronet, bandeau, necklace, stomacher, and bracelet—that the sixth duke had made for Countess Granville, wife of his nephew, to wear in Moscow for the coronation of Alexander II. Always known as the Devonshire parure, and epitomizing the English neo-Renaissance style, it was shown at the International Exhibition of 1862, when the *Gazette des Beaux Arts* praised it as being "*d'un grand gout et d'une excellente composition.*" All the largest diamonds were removed in 1892 and set in a new tiara for the duchess of Devonshire of the day, but the parure, which is otherwise intact, is now displayed in the private apartments of the duke and duchess at Chatsworth.

The Devonshire parure from the catalogue of the London International Exhibition (1862), when it was exhibited by C. F. Hancock. The parure, consisting of tiara, coronet, comb, bandeau, bracelet, necklace, and V-shaped stomacher brooch, is set with ancient and Renaissance cameos and intaglios.

MUSEUM OF FINE ARTS, BOSTON

DEVONSHIRE TIARA 1856 C.F. HANCOCK, ENGLISH
Gold, enamel, diamonds, cameos, intaglios.

• • •

From a band of bead-and-reel pattern rises a series of plaques, each filled with minute flowers and leaves and bordered at the top by palmettes, enameled in various colors and interspersed with beads. The tiara is inspired by the original Greek (third–second century B.C.) model in the collection of the Marchese Campana of Rome, acquired by Napoleon III for the Louvre (1861). E. Fontenay, himself a jeweler, admired it in *Les Bijoux Anciens et Modernes* (1887) "on account of the exceptional finesse of the goldwork, universally acknowledged," but went on to criticize the excess of detail that detracted from the overall effect: a tiara, he said, should impress from a distance, and therefore required a bold outline, not demanding close examination. Pioneers of the archaeological revival style, Fortunato Pio Castellani (1794–1864) and his son, Augusto (1829–1914), adapted the designs and techniques of the ancient Etruscan, Greek, and Roman goldsmiths to modern use. Their shop in the Palazzo Poli in Rome was visited by all who went to that city as pilgrims or as tourists, and as well as setting up branches in Paris and London, they took stands at the international exhibitions.

THE SATALOFF AND CLUCHEY FAMILY

The gold band is outlined at the base with beading and is centered on two, octofoil medallions surmounted by a smaller one, flanked by another four to each side. The smaller medallions on each side enclose mosaics of plants and flowers within quatrefoils, and that at the top encloses a scarab. Mosaics of doves of peace, facing outward and framed in palmettes, are set in the two octofoils. The dove, copied from a mosaic in one of the early Christian churches in Rome, was a favorite choice for jewelry in the mid-nineteenth century. The poet Elizabeth Barrett Browning (1806–61) wears a brooch with the mosaic dove motif in her portrait by Michele Gordigiani (now at the Philadelphia Museum of Art), and in a letter to the wife of the sculptor, Mrs. William Wetmore Story, she expresses her attachment to this Christian symbol, "so significant and touching to us all." The gold setting, decorated with corded wire and beading, along with the use of glass mosaics, is in the "Etruscan" style, made fashionable by the success of the archaeological jewelry pioneered by Castellani of Rome. Since the makers exported unmounted mosaics, it is difficult to attribute a place of origin to the gold setting, but the beading and filigree are also characteristic of Roman work.

ALBION ART, JAPAN

↑ ARCHAEOLOGICAL REVIVAL TIARA   1860s   CASTELLANI, ITALIAN   ↓ PEACE TIARA   1860s   MOSAICS ROMAN, SETTING ENGLISH (?)
Gold, enamel, agate, glass beads.   Gold, glass, mosaics.

• •

From a base of collet-set diamonds rise convergent and divergent scrolls surmounted by large diamonds. The grandeur of this fender design is matched by the distinguished provenance: the collection of Grand Duchess Vladimir, born Duchess Marie of Mecklenburg-Schwerin, married to the uncle of Tsar Nicholas II and a dominant figure at his court. Connoisseur of pearls, emeralds, and diamonds, she bought with great discrimination from Russian and Parisian jewelers, encouraging Cartier and Chaumet to do business in St. Petersburg. This sumptuous tiara illustrates the excellent taste of a rich, intelligent, and supremely royal lady.

PRIVATE COLLECTION

THE GRAND DUCHESS VLADIMIR'S TIARA C. 1870 RUSSIAN
Gold, silver, diamonds.

The halo-shaped tiara is bordered by brilliant-cut diamonds at the base and the top, and the space between is filled in with seven large cabochon emeralds in diamond frames, divided by diamond latticework. The emeralds belonged to Marie of Hesse, wife of Tsar Alexander II, and then to her daughter-in-law, Princess Elizabeth of Hesse, wife of the Grand Duke Serge, but the date of the tiara itself is uncertain. Following the assassination of the Grand Duke Serge in 1905, the grand duchess retired from public life and founded the religious order of Martha and Mary. Some of her jewels were sold; others were entrusted to her brother-in-law, the Grand Duke Paul. He went into exile, and the Grand Duchess Serge brought up his daughter, the Grand Duchess Marie. When the Grand Duchess Marie married in 1908, she received the tiara and matching necklace as a gift from her aunt. While in exile in Romania with her second husband, she sold them in 1922 to Alexander II of Yugoslavia for his bride, Princess Marie of Romania. The bride's mother, Queen Marie of Romania, described the emeralds as "imperial stones the like of which I hadn't seen since Russia." Whereas the necklace was remodeled by Cartier, the tiara has remained intact. The queen of Yugoslavia wore it for most of her official portraits and took it into exile with her, allowing her daughter-in-law, Alexandra, wife of King Peter II, to borrow it only once for a reception in Buckingham Palace in honor of the marriage of the future Queen Elizabeth II. Queen Alexandra recalled in *For a King's Love* (1956): "My head ached and hurt unbearably under the weight of the heavy tiara of emeralds which I wore . . . my tiara bit viciously into my head." In 1949 the tiara was sold to Van Cleef & Arpels, who removed the emeralds but kept the rest.

VAN CLEEF & ARPELS, PARIS

Queen Marie of Yugoslavia wearing the emerald and diamond tiara bought for her by Alexander II at the time of their marriage in 1922.

THE ILLUSTRATED LONDON NEWS PICTURE LIBRARY

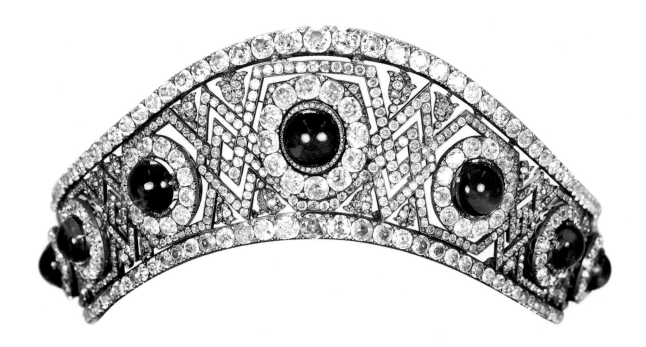

THE QUEEN OF SERBIA'S TIARA 1800s BOLIN, RUSSIAN
Gold, silver, diamonds, paste replacement for emeralds.

The tiara rests on a continuous line of close-set diamonds supporting an open-work band of navette-shaped links enclosing three collet-set stones between verticals also of three collet-set stones. This band, dating to the late eighteenth century, is surmounted by a sequence of alternately low and high spikes graduated in height toward the back. The two elements were combined for the wife of the fourth Earl Howe, presumably at the time of her marriage (1883). They lived at the heart of London society, entertaining the royal family at Curzon House in Mayfair and at their country estate, Gopsall, in Leicestershire. In full dress, long diamond earrings, her grandest diamond necklace, and with this tiara on her head, she rode in the Howe family coach to Buckingham Palace or to the state opening of Parliament, accompanied by footmen in state livery and driven by a coachman wearing a three-cornered hat over his wig.

The continuous line of diamonds at the base supports a sequence of alternate wide and high pavéd and narrow and low collet-set spikes radiating upward in a sun-ray design. Of Russian inspiration, the sun ray, fringe, or spike is one of the most successful tiaras, worn internationally from St. Petersburg to New York. This example was probably one of the jewels given to the Infanta Maria Theresa of Portugal (1855–1944) when she became the third wife of the Archduke Charles Louis, brother of the Emperor Francis Joseph of Austria, in 1873. After the death of the Empress Elizabeth and the second marriage of the crown princess, she was often seen at the side of the emperor at court ceremonies wearing this tiara, notably at the wedding of the Archduke Charles with Princess Zita of Bourbon Parme (1911). It passed to her daughter, Elizabeth Amelie (1878–1960), who married Prince Aloys de Liechtenstein (1903) and it has since been worn by several generations of that family, including Princess Gina, wife of Prince Francis Joseph II, and the brides of Prince Hans Adam (1967) and Prince Philippe Erasmus (1971).

Yevonde photograph (1930) of Mary, first wife of the fifth Earl Howe, wearing the spike tiara.

↑ HOWE TIARA 1883 ENGLISH
Gold, silver, diamonds.

↓ LIECHTENSTEIN TIARA C. 1875 ATTRIBUTED TO KÖCHERT, AUSTRIAN
Gold, silver, diamonds.

This tiara, by the Russian court jeweler Fabergé, rests on a base enameled pale blue *en guilloche* imitating a ribbon of moiré silk, and is surmounted by a sequence of leafy scrolls, slanting toward the back to each side of a pointed cinquefoil enclosing a bunch of stylized lilies, flanked by buds on stems. The unusual feature of this design, which combines the technique of enameling with that of stone setting, is the blue bandeau that matched the color of the eyes and dress of the wearer. It illustrates the international appeal of the garland style, which extended from Paris to London to New York and across Europe to Moscow, where this was purchased. For other Fabergé tiaras, see A. K. Snowman, *Fabergé: Lost and Found* (1993).

RUSSIAN-STYLE GARLAND TIARA C. 1910 FABERGÉ, RUSSIAN
Platinum, enamel, diamonds.

The three-layered sun, rays tipped with diamonds, is centered on a gray pearl. The motif, an elaboration of the Russian spike tiara, lends itself particularly well to the display of the diamonds glittering in the sunbeams. Famous examples were made by Cartier for J. P. Morgan (1904) and the American-born countess of Suffolk, and by Joseph Chaumet for Princess Youssoupoff (1914). It looked equally striking whether worn high or low on the head or taken off the frame to pin to the bodice.

The tall halo-shaped tiara rests on two continuous lines of channel-set diamonds with a row of collet-set stones between, with a curved channel-set top border. The inside of the halo is filled with a row of collet-set stones above the base to each side of channel-set curvilinear motifs topped by collet-set stones. Above rises a network of diamonds on knife-edge supports as fine as lace. The résille, or mesh pattern, was not only used for tiaras, as here, but also for elaborate necklaces such as that made by Cartier for Queen Alexandra (1904).

THOMAS FÄRBER

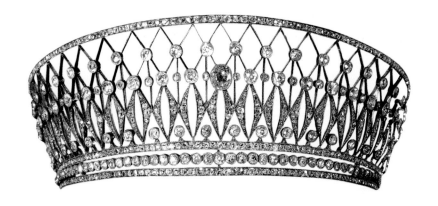

↑ TRIPLE-SUN TIARA C. 1910 FRENCH
Platinum, brilliants, gray pearl.

↓ MESH-PATTERN HALO C. 1910 RUSSIAN
Platinum millegrain, diamonds.

The halo-shaped tiara rests on a band of alternate large and small pearls between lines of channel-set diamonds, repeated in the upper border, which is surmounted at intervals by small collet-set stones. The space within is filled by fifteen pear-shaped diamond drops hanging from stylized buds between pearls above and below. The drops swinging freely would catch the light to great effect as the wearer moved her head. Although sometimes associated with neo-classical designs, the tiara was described as a "diadème russe" by Cartier because the halo shape is so close to that of the *kokoshnik.*

CARTIER

"RUSSIAN" TIARA 1908 CARTIER, FRENCH
Platinum millegrain, diamonds, pearls.

The *kokoshnik*-style tiara, which rests on a line of diamonds with a second line of *calibré*-cut rubies above, is bordered at the top by further ruby and diamond borders, rising to a peak. The space between is filled with pear-shaped diamonds framed in *calibré*-cut rubies between pairs of circular-cut, collet-set diamonds standing out against a ground of blackened steel. It is one of six similar designs using blackened steel recorded in the Cartier archives, all with different patterns applied. This tiara was ordered by Madame Marghiloman, wife of the Romanian statesman and prime minister.

CARTIER

MARGHILOMAN TIARA 1914 CARTIER, FRENCH
Steel, platinum, rubies, diamonds.

The base and top of the tiara are outlined by channel-set diamonds enclosing a continuous line of ribbons, with the space between filled with seven octagonal emeralds within open oval frames graduated in size toward the back. These are surmounted by groups of collet-set diamonds and supported below by leafy sprays joined to the stems of flowers linking the emeralds. These emeralds have an interesting provenance: they descended from the sister of the banker, J. Pierpont Morgan, Mary Hayes Burns, to her daughter Mary, who married Lewis, first Viscount Harcourt, in 1899, and the tiara probably dates from their wedding.

PRIVATE COLLECTION

Hayes Wrightson photograph of Viscountess Harcourt (1937) dressed in her robes for the coronation of George VI with the emerald and diamond tiara on her head and the Harcourt necklace made for her by Cartier (1920).

PRIVATE COLLECTION

THE HARCOURT TIARA C. 1900 ENGLISH (?)
Gold, silver, emeralds, diamonds.

THE IVEAGH TIARA C. 1900 R.S. GARRARD, ENGLISH
Gold, silver, diamonds.
See page 122

TALHOUET TIARA   C. 1908   JOSEPH CHAUMET, FRENCH
Gold, silver, diamonds.
See page 122

• •

BOWKNOT TIARA C. 1900 JOSEPH CHAUMET, FRENCH
Gold, silver, pink topazes, diamonds.
See page 123

LEAFY-SPRAY TIARA c. 1905 ENGLISH
Platinum, diamonds, pearls.
See page 123

••

From a continuous line of channel-set diamonds encircling the head rise tall curvilinear elements enclosing collet-set diamonds on knife-edge supports, which give additional height to the design. Light but imposing, this all-around crown has been worn during this century by the wives of the first, second, and third earls of Iveagh. In 1906, the first Lady Iveagh brought a party from her country house, Elveden, to a ball given by Earl Cadogan: she was wearing white with ropes of pearls and this crown placed high on hair dressed "à la Marquise."

The tiara is set with diamonds throughout in a rich pattern of continuous vine scrolls, meeting at a central cushion-shaped diamond framed within leafy scrolls. This pattern, which derives from wrought-iron decorating Parisian architecture in the Louis XVI style, was extremely popular, and Chaumet made several versions of it. This tiara was made for the Marquise de Talhouet.

The lower edge of the tiara is formed by ribbons in swags tied at intervals into bowknots surmounted by leafy sprays tipped with diamonds. Between the bows are vertical elements studded with pink topazes and joined together by festoons of collet diamonds overlapping the ribbon swags below. There is a line of collet-set diamonds above. The combination of swags, festoons, ribbons, bowknots, and leaves is in the eighteenth-century tradition, revived as the "garland style" in the Belle Epoque.

CHAUMET, PARIS

The curved base of the tiara rises toward the center, which is surmounted by volutes flanked on each side by a sequence of graduated leafy sprays, each tipped with a pearl. The light and delicate design is an excellent example of the fashionable garland style.

PRIVATE COLLECTION

The tiara rests on a line of channel-set brilliants and is surmounted by another border, similarly set, rising to a point in the center with a trefoil above and smaller trefoils at intervals to each side. The space between is filled with running scrolls interspersed with trefoils meeting at a figure of eight in the middle. This grand design, typical of Chaumet, compares with a nickel silver replica in that firm's collection of tiara models. It was worn by the first Countess Mountbatten of Burma to the many formal events she attended as a relation by marriage to George V, George VI, and Elizabeth II, and the duke of Edinburgh. While her husband officiated as viceroy and then governor general of India, (1947–48), she alternated it with another tiara of pearls and diamonds because, according to her daughter, "she could not be seen twice in the same one."

THE LADY PAMELA HICKS

Yevonde photograph (1937) of the future Countess Mountbatten of Burma in lamé evening dress and tiara.

MOUNTBATTEN ARCHIVE, SOUTHAMPTON UNIVERSITY LIBRARY

MOUNTBATTEN TIARA c. 1910 FRENCH
Platinum millegrain, diamonds.

• •

A line of collet-set stones rise to a point in the center of the tiara, and the top is bordered by trails of laurel. The wide space between is filled with vine scrolls and stylized buds converging on a 5.84-carat diamond in the center. The running-scroll motif, combined with the laurel trail and the shape, echoes the tiaras of the first part of the nineteenth century.

CARTIER

Speaight photograph (1921) of the queen of the Belgians. Born Princess Elizabeth of Bavaria, she married the future Albert I in 1900: he became king in 1909. An art lover, talented musician, and sculptor, she was beloved by her subjects. Here the tiara is worn "à la Josephine," low on the brow with court dress.

THE ILLUSTRATED LONDON NEWS
PICTURE LIBRARY

QUEEN OF THE BELGIANS TIARA 1910 CARTIER, FRENCH
Platinum millegrain, diamonds.

• •

The tiara, which rests on a wreath of stylized laurel between a line of running scrolls and an upper row of square and rectangular cut stones, is surmounted by a curved line of channel-set diamonds interspersed with stones set lozenge-wise rising to a point at the center. The space between is filled with intersecting Louis XVI–style festoons and swags, which hang with freely swinging open-set diamonds. Although the front of the tiara is platinum, the back is executed in yellow gold. It was probably made for the coronation of Grand Duke Friedrich II (1907), and thereafter Grand Duchess Hilda (1864–1952), born a princess of Luxembourg, always wore this tiara on great occasions such as the eightieth birthday party of the king of Sweden (1938). Since she had no children, she left her jewels to the six daughters of her brother, Grand Duke William IV: the tiara, which went to Antoinette, wife of Prince Rupert of Bavaria, was later acquired by the Badisches Landesmuseum (1984). It has thus returned to the palace, where it was worn very often by Grand Duchess Hilda for the first fifty years of this century.

BADISCHES LANDESMUSEUM, KARLSRUHE

Grand Duchess Hilda, wife of Grand Duke Friedrich II of Baden, wearing the Louis XVI–style diamond tiara high at the back of her coiffure (1907).

BADISCHES LANDESMUSEUM, KARLSRUHE

GRAND DUCHESS HILDA'S TIARA 1907 SCHMIDT-STAUB OF PFORZHEIM, GERMAN
Platinum, gold, diamonds.

• •

GARLAND-STYLE TIARA 1909 CARTIER, FRENCH
Platinum millegrain, diamonds.
See page 134

• •

LAUREL TIARA C. 1900 ENGLISH
Gold, silver, diamonds.
See page 135

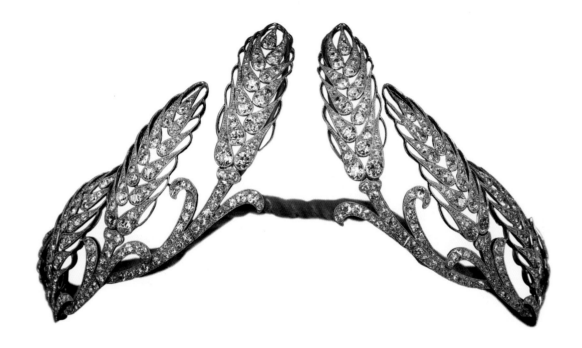

WHEAT-EAR TIARA   c. 1910   FRENCH (?)
Platinum millegrain, diamonds.
See page 135

• •

The base of the tiara consists of a line of collet-set diamonds, terminating in curved ends, and the top is bordered by a delicate wreath of laurel, meeting at a collet-set diamond in the center. The space between is filled in with a sequence of graduated ovals of collet-set diamonds enclosing pear-shaped diamonds swinging loosely from foliate scrolls, within channel-set frames. Between each oval are collet-set roundels with stylized buds above and below. Light and delicate, this tiara, with its use of laurel, scrolls, and stylized buds, channel- and collet-set diamonds, illustrates the Cartier garland style. The movement of the pear-shaped diamonds was an innovation, previously associated with single stone earrings rather than with tiaras.

ALBION ART, JAPAN

The tiara, which can also be worn as a necklace, is mounted on a frame from which rise five open-work, heart-shaped scroll motifs, set with cushion-shaped and rose diamonds, each enclosing a large collet-set diamond and surmounted by two others, that in the center by a later top cluster, linked by festoons of collet-set stones. The design exemplifies the elegance of the garland style, which is based on eighteenth-century models. Here, the heart-shaped scrolls echo the center of the tiara made for Viscountess Montagu in 1767, which is an heirloom of the Spencer family. Cartier used the same motif for the *kokoshnik* tiara of Lina Cavalieri, "the loveliest prima donna in the world" (*Tatler*, 1909). This tiara, which was made for the wife of a Russian diplomat using stones from the family collection and others removed from a decoration, probably the Nashami-al-Imtiaz presented by the Sultan Abdul Hamid II (1876–1909), has been in the family ever since. It was ordered in St. Petersburg, and executed in Paris.

PRIVATE COLLECTION

The tiara is a wreath of twin branches of laurel leaves and berries meeting at the center, with a large collet-set diamond hanging between them. For the ancient Greeks, the laurel was sacred to Apollo, and, awarded to the victors of games and musical contests held in his honor, it became a symbol of triumph. For this reason, laurel leaf tiaras were worn by both the Emperor Napoleon and the Empress Josephine at their coronation in 1804, and again during the Second Empire by the Empress Eugènie, wife of Napoleon III. During the first part of the twentieth century, the laurel was one of the favorite themes for tiaras made by Cartier for Mrs. George Keppel, the favorite of Edward VII (1904), the American Comtesse de Castellane (née Anna Gould), Lady Astor, and Mrs. Eva Stotesbury. A later version was made for the queen of Spain, also by Cartier.

ALBION ART, JAPAN

The wheat ears set throughout with diamonds follow the contours of the head to meet above the forehead. Derived from antiquity, the motif of wheat ears sacred to Ceres, goddess of the harvest, symbolizes prosperity. The beautiful sister of Napoleon, Princess Pauline Borghese, attended his coronation in 1804 with a tiara of this design, which remained in fashion through-out the nineteenth century. This version, executed in platinum, has a more realistic, light, "blown in the wind" quality that could not be achieved by craftsmen using the heavier gold and silver settings.

PRIVATE COLLECTION

The Greek-key pattern, the theme of this tiara, is curved and not angular, which is the more usual form. Joseph Chaumet made several versions of this model, chosen by women who wanted a classical design but found the straight "meander" lines too cold and hard. This curvilinear alternative was easier to wear and much more flattering to the features.

The Greek-key pattern is entwined with delicate trails of leaves to soften the severity of the angular outline. For the pattern to be shown to greater effect, the bandeau might also be mounted on a velvet ribbon. The motif from antiquity reflects the fashion for neoclassical jewelry during the years leading up to World War I. This model was particularly favored by French women, who placed them far back on the head so as to show off their coiffures. Made for Mademoiselle de Grammont upon her marriage with the Marquis de Labriffe, the bandeau is still owned by her descendants.

Lallie Charles photograph (1908) of Lady Juliet Duff wearing her Greek-key pattern bandeau with feathers high on her head.

↑ KEY PATTERN TIARA 1913 JOSEPH CHAUMET, FRENCH   ↓ LABRIFFE BANDEAU 1914 JOSEPH CHAUMET, FRENCH
Platinum millegrain, diamonds.   Platinum, diamonds.

The bandeau from the Parisian firm of Boucheron consists of two narrow bands with foliage between roundels, finished with a circular plaque at each end. Flexible and adjustable, it can be worn Empire style low on the brow or rest on the back of the head as desired. It can also be converted to other purposes such as a shoulder ornament. The light foliage and graceful curves are in tune with the classical spirit of the art of the Louis XVI period revived in the final years of the Belle Epoque.

ALBION ART, JAPAN

The tiara consists of a frame surmounted by a pair of wings, feathers closely set with diamonds, and patches of translucent blue enamel. They are adjustable to any angle and can be taken off the frame to wear as brooches, individually or as a pair. The motif was inspired by the winged helmets worn by the flying Valkyries in the operas of Richard Wagner, which attracted large audiences. To honor the composer, Wagner nights were always "tiara nights" at the Paris and London opera houses. This pair matches the description of the wings entered for stock in 1907 and bought by the Duke of Westminster from Chaumet that year. Wings had a long run: Cartier supplied a pair to the duchess of Roxburghe in 1935, the last of a series that had begun in 1899.

THOMAS FÄRBER

↑ DOUBLE BANDEAU C. 1912 BOUCHERON, FRENCH
Platinum millegrain, diamonds.

↓ VALKYRIE WING TIARA 1907 JOSEPH CHAUMET, FRENCH
Platinum, diamonds, translucent blue enamel.

The open-work pattern of geometric motifs rises to the peak in the center, which is emphasized by a Persian palmette, all executed in diamonds. The evenly geometric outline and the Persian palmette are characteristic of Art Deco, a style based on Asian elements subordinated to the strict discipline of mathematics. The bandeau is divisible into two wide bracelets.

CARTIER

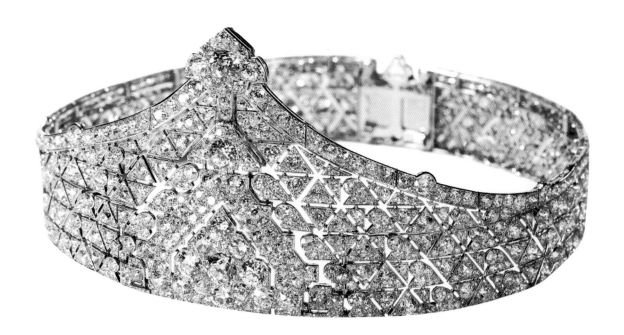

PERSIAN BANDEAU 1923 CARTIER, FRENCH
Platinum millegrain, diamonds.

• •

BOURBON PARME TIARA 1919 JOSEPH CHAUMET, FRENCH
Platinum millegrain, diamonds.
See page 146

TIARA
• •

DIVERGENT SCROLL TIARA   c. 1930   BULGARI, ITALIAN
Platinum, diamonds.
See page 146

• • •

TOPAZ BANDEAU 1937 CARTIER, LONDON
Platinum, gold, dark and light topazes.
See page 147

The base, consisting of alternate large and small collet-set diamonds, is surmounted by leafy sprays on knife-edge stems, each with a pear-shaped diamond at the tip, and hung with both circular-cut and pear-shaped stones. This tall tiara, which is in the grand tradition of the Belle Epoque, was commissioned by the duchess de La Rochefoucauld as a present for her daughter, Hedwige (1896–1986), on her marriage to Prince Sixte of Bourbon Parme. The conservative design and height were acceptable to royal taste and seems to have pleased the owner, who wore it until the end of her life.

THOMAS FÄRBER

The line of close-set diamonds at the base is surmounted by a succession of scrolls back-to-back, each pair supporting a pear-shaped diamond between two navette-shaped diamonds. The point at which the scrolls meet below is marked by a collet-set round diamond. The conservative design by Bulgari, which echoes the early-nineteenth-century tiaras of the First Empire, is in tune with the fashion for "all-white" jewelry of the 1930s, as are the sharp cuts of the diamonds. In spite of the huge success of this Roman jeweler, tiaras were rarely executed. This example may have been ordered for the marriage of Princess Marie José of Belgium with the future Umberto II in the chapel of the Quirinal Palace (1930), when the bride wore the magnificent "fender" of Queen Margherita over her Brussels-lace veil, and the guests wore their tiaras, not only to the wedding, but to the other festivities celebrating it.

ALBION ART, JAPAN

The three young women are wearing tiaras suited to the short hair and tunic dresses of the 1920s. One tiara is of scrollwork design rising to a peak, the second is of half circles with a trail of leaves running through them, and the third is a double flat bandeaux. All are worn "à la Josephine," low on the forehead.

CHAUMET, PARIS

A band of baton-cut light and dark topazes rise to a centerpiece detachable as a clip brooch. This motif is set with a large, light-colored topaz (62.15 carat) framed within dark baton- and hexagonal-cut topazes bordered by diamonds. The size of the topaz makes for a splendid effect, at moderate price, and the sprinkling of diamonds does not detract from the mass of golden color. Topaz was a favorite stone of Jacques Cartier, for many years director of Cartier, London, who, after buying a large consignment of these stones, announced to his design studio, "Now, we are going to have some fun!" Because of the lower cost, Cartier could be more experimental with topaz and aquamarine than with precious stones.

CARTIER

The tiara comprises a narrow band of close-set diamonds surmounted in the center by curved elements framing a double oval frame bordering a large marquise diamond, flanked on each side by latticework, terminating in smaller curvilinear elements. The diamond was a gift from the board of de Beers when the earl of Bessborough retired to take up a new appointment as governor general of Canada. The tiara is an excellent example of the fusion of tradition with modernity, for while the proportions are impressive, the linear design strikes a contemporary note, which the wearer, who was described in fashion magazines of the time as having "all the charm and chic of a smart French woman," would have required.

MARY, COUNTESS OF BESSBOROUGH

Yousuf Karsh photograph (1931) of the countess of Bessborough wearing her tiara and a silver lamé Worth gown.

MARY, COUNTESS OF BESSBOROUGH

Mrs. Joseph Kennedy, wife of the U.S. ambassador, dressed for her presentation at court (1938). In her autobiography, *Times to Remember* (1974), she wrote, "As a matron I would wear a tiara in my hair. I didn't own one. It had simply never occurred to me before coming to England that I would ever need one. My new and sympathetic friend Lady Bessborough lent me hers and it proved to be exactly right, most flattering and magnificent. (It fitted very well and had many brilliant diamonds including a gorgeous marquise diamond in the front. With a few temporary adjustments and arrangements it was perfect. I was so grateful to her for the thought. I remember my children—Bobby and Teddy as well as the girls—were extremely impressed.)"

JOHN F. KENNEDY LIBRARY

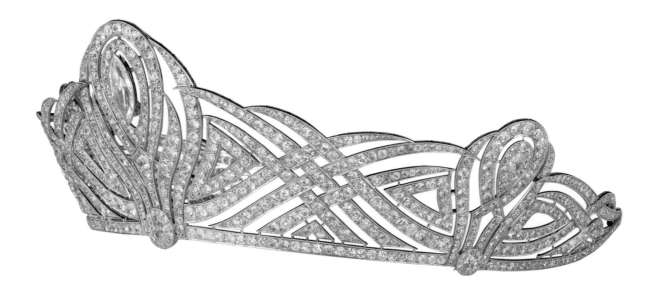

BESSBOROUGH TIARA   1931   JOSEPH CHAUMET, FRENCH
Platinum, diamonds.

The tiara rests on a detachable projecting band of geometric ornament set with baguette and brilliant-cut diamonds from which rises a halo of lotus flowers alternating with buds and terminating with an incurved bud at each end. Representing the Egyptian style, which was one of Cartier's great successes of the interwar period, the lotus is interpreted in an all-white design using diamonds of different cuts. Made for stock, this tiara was bought by H. H. Aga Khan III for his wife, Andrée, whom he married in 1929.

CARTIER

Photograph by Fayer of Vienna of the Begum Aga Khan (1935) wearing her lotus halo with evening dress and other jewelry. A leading racehorse owner, the Aga Khan was very well known to London society, and Princess Andrée's jewels, particularly her emeralds, always made a great impression.

THE ILLUSTRATED LONDON NEWS
PICTURE LIBRARY

EGYPTIAN STYLE TIARA 1934 CARTIER, LONDON
Platinum, diamonds.

The tiara rests on a double line of oval aquamarines surmounted by nine graduated motifs in aquamarines and brilliants, two oval aquamarines between them. The central motif is detachable for wear as a clip brooch. Since this is one of the twenty-seven tiaras made by Cartier, London in 1937, it was probably worn at the many social events held in connection with the coronation of George VI, which took place that year. The baton cut gives a new look to the aquamarine, which is well suited to the fashionable abstract design.

The staircase of the Paris opera with women in evening dress and halo-shaped tiaras as rendered by J. Simont for *L'Illustration* (1934).

AQUAMARINE TIARA 1937 CARTIER, LONDON
Platinum, aquamarines, diamonds.

• •
153

The tiara is in the form of a garland centered on an eight-petalled flower with convolvuli to each side entirely set with diamonds, mounted on trembler springs. It is also part of a set that includes two brooches. The botanical theme, first revived by Chaumet/Fossin around 1820 to recapture the spirit of pre-Revolutionary French art, was adopted internationally and has been a favorite in England ever since. The traditional "romantic" character appealed to Mrs. Marjorie Merriweather Post, who acquired the tiara from the collection of Lord Methuen (1970), in whose family it had presumably descended from the first owner.

SMITHSONIAN INSTITUTION, WASHINGTON, DC

Mrs. Post wearing one of the tiaras from her collection (c.1950).

HILLWOOD MUSEUM, WASHINGTON, D.C.

FLORAL TIARA Mid 1800s ENGLISH
Gold, silver, diamonds.

• •

KEMP TIARA 1894 TIFFANY & CO., AMERICAN
Gold, platinum, diamonds.
See page 160

TIARA
• •
156

BRAND TIARA 1935 CARTIER, LONDON
Platinum, turquoises, diamonds.
See page 160

•••

OAK LEAF BANDEAU 1920 JOSEPH CHAUMET, FRENCH
Platinum, diamonds.
See page 161

ESSEX TIARA   1902   CARTIER, FRENCH
Silver, gold, diamonds.
See page 161

• •

The tiara, which consists of a sequence of overlapping pairs of C scrolls surmounted by trefoils and enclosing plant motifs, is entirely set with pear-shaped and circular-cut diamonds. It is inscribed "JULIA FROM HER MOTHER, JUNE 6, 1894." Julia Kemp left it to her sister Marion, who lived in Rome for most of her 104 years, and she in her turn bequeathed it to the mother of the present owner.

PRIVATE COLLECTION

The tiara consists of a continuous line of diamonds surmounted by two tiers of carved turquoise Indian palm leaves and buds meeting at a central motif of two buds in diamond caps and terminating in scrolled ends. Presumably ordered for the festivities marking the Silver Jubilee of George V, by Phyllis Brand, née Langhorne of Virginia (1880–1937), it exemplifies the taste for Asian motifs in the interwar period. Tall, with dark hair and good looks, Phyllis was the favorite sister of Nancy Viscountess Astor and lived in England after her marriage to R. H. Brand, public servant and banker, in 1917.

CARTIER

The bandeau consists of a series of interlaced crowns of oak leaves, enclosing ovals of collet-set stones. It can also be clasped round the neck as a collar. Made for a wedding present, it was ordered by Baroness Hottinguer, née Marian Munroe of Boston, wife of a member of the famous French banking family. The graceful design is in the garland style, which continued to appeal well into the interwar period.

PRIVATE COLLECTION

The tiara consists of a series of scrolls divergent at the center and surmounted by nine collet-set diamonds between the curves. The countess of Essex, née Adela Beach Grant of New York, married the earl of Essex in 1893. *Tatler* (1908) described her in a profile portrait: "Tall and graceful, with soft eyes, dark hair, a 'magnolia' complexion, always turned out to perfection in the best of Paris gowns … never overloaded with jewels … dainty and graceful … at the royal balls and the smartest parties." She wore the tiara to the coronation of Edward VII (1902), and it was lent to Clementine, wife of Sir Winston Churchill, for that of Elizabeth II (1953).

CARTIER

The tiara is a gold wreath of laurel leaves and berries, inspired by those worn as a symbol of victory by the ancient Greeks and Romans. It is inscribed "TO VIRA BOARMAN WHITEHOUSE FROM THE WOMEN OF NEW YORK STATE WHOM SHE LED TO VICTORY, NOVEMBER 1917." This refers to her leadership of the movement for women's enfranchisement, which was won in the New York state elections that year. Although a suffrage bill had been presented annually ever since the Civil War, the opposition was so entrenched that it never got further than the committee stage. Mrs. Whitehouse (1875–1957) devoted herself to this cause with formidable energy: publicizing it, rebutting all antisuffrage articles and correspondence in the press, and then, as chairman of the New York Woman Suffrage Party, raising the funds necessary to finance the final year of the campaign.

PRIVATE COLLECTION, NEW YORK

The photograph of Mrs. Whitehouse with her dog, Sonny, by Ernest Walter Histead, shows her much as she must have looked, "young, beautiful and brimful of energy" when leading the campaign for women's votes in the New York state elections. In token of her victory, she was presented by her supporters with the tiara at right.

THE MUSEUM OF THE CITY OF NEW YORK

VICTORY TIARA 1917 AMERICAN
Gold.

• •

The bandeau is centered on a checkerboard motif of stepped outline, set with an oriental pearl and surmounted by two pear-shaped diamonds. Similar motifs are on each side graduated toward the back, alternating with geometric-pattern vertical elements. This striking design, which belonged to the tobacco heiress Doris Duke, was worn flat on the sleek short hair and with the long earrings fashionable in the 1920s.

DORIS DUKE CHARITABLE FOUNDATION

Cecil Beaton photograph of
Doris Duke (c. 1930).

DORIS DUKE CHARITABLE FOUNDATION

DORIS DUKE BANDEAU C. 1930 CARTIER, FRENCH
Platinum, diamonds, pearl.

• •

Bunched into two groups, from a convex gold band rise feathers, some with diamonds, others with diamonds set into a tapering center vein. Inspired by the feathered headdress of Native Americans, Fulco di Verdura (1898–1978) made this for Mrs. John Hay Whitney to wear as wife of the U.S. ambassador to the Court of St. James. Executed in gold rather than in cold, white platinum as was Verdura's preference, the bold and original design illustrates his talent for expressing traditional symbolism in the language of the New World.

VERDURA, NEW YORK

Mrs. and Mrs. John Hay Whitney on their arrival in London, 1956. She was Betsey, one of the three daughters (along with Babe Paley and Minnie Astor Fosburgh) of Dr. Harvey Cushing, world-famous Boston neurosurgeon.

AP/WIDE WORLD PHOTOS

WHITNEY TIARA   1957   FULCO DI VERDURA, ITALIAN (WORKED FRANCE AND AMERICA)
Gold, diamonds.

• • •

The base, composed of a continuous line of collet-set, circular-cut brilliants, is surmounted by a graduated series of vertical elements mounted with pear-shaped, navette, and circular-cut diamonds. The light from each of these cuts contributes a different accent to the overall design. The minimal flexible setting is easily convertible to wear as a necklace. Princess Grace, who wore this tiara to the wedding of her eldest daughter, Princess Caroline, in 1978, was a long-standing customer of Van Cleef & Arpels. The firm supplied the diamond-and-pearl parure, which Prince Rainier of Monaco gave her as a present upon their marriage (1956), and was awarded the appointment of jewelers to the principality.

VAN CLEEF & ARPELS, PARIS

Princess Grace dancing with the Aga Khan at a ball in 1960, tiara on her head.

PRIVATE COLLECTION

PRINCESS GRACE TIARA 1976 VAN CLEEF & ARPELS, FRENCH
Platinum, diamonds.

Mrs. Cornelius Vanderbilt II (c.1890).

PRESERVATION SOCIETY OF NEWPORT COUNTY

Mrs. Cornelius Vanderbilt III (c.1900).

PRESERVATION SOCIETY OF NEWPORT COUNTY

Countess Nostitz wearing her ruby
and diamond Chaumet tiara (1907).

PRIVATE COLLECTION

Mrs. W.B. Leeds wearing her Cartier tiara (1917).

Baron Adolph de Meyer photograph for *Vogue* of Mrs. Harry Payne Whitney (1917).

The Countess of Galloway dressed for the coronation of George VI (1937).

The tiara consists of three diamond stems with leaves of carved horn, dyed russet brown, curving gently across into an asymmetrical pattern. As a proponent of Art Nouveau, René Lalique (1860–1945) proposed a fresh approach to the tiara. His inspiration is Japanese rather than European naturalism, and his use of horn carved to different degrees of transparency conveys the autumnal character of the leaves far more effectively than pearls or diamonds could. His genius led him to create jewels like this, that are works of art, complete in themselves, but that were also intended for wear. The color of these leaves would sit well above the rich brown henna-dyed hair of the rather theatrical type of beauty suited to Lalique's particular vision.

VIRGINIA MUSEUM OF FINE ARTS, RICHMOND

AUTUMN TIARA C. 1900 RENÉ LALIQUE, FRENCH
Gold, horn, diamonds, tortoiseshell.

••

FOLIATE BANDEAU 1910 GEORGES FOUQUET, FRENCH
Gold, silver, enamel, diamonds, aquamarines.
See page 178

WINGED GLOBE TIARA c. 1900 CHILD AND CHILD, ENGLISH
Silver, enamel, citrine.
See page 178

GOTHIC TIARA c. 1910 HENRY WILSON, ENGLISH
Gold, enamel, diamonds, sapphires, citrine.
See page 179

TIARA
• •

DOLPHIN TIARA   c. 1900   JAMES CROMAR WATT, SCOTTISH
Silver, enamel, freshwater pearls.
See page 179

The narrow bandeau, tapering toward the ends, is bordered above and below by a continuous line of collet-set diamonds, and the space between is filled by a wreath of *plique à jour* enameled leaves, studded with oval aquamarines at intervals. It is very close in style to another equally neat and simplified bandeau (illustrated by M. N. de Gary, *Les Fouquet*, 1983, p. 92). Both are decorated with this type of enamel and embellished with aquamarines, the jeweler's favorite stones, which led to his nickname "Le Père de l'aigue-marine" in the gem trade. Like Lalique, Georges Fouquet (1862–1957) chose to rely on the artistic quality of his designs and technique rather than on expensive materials. This example shows how he adapted the principles of Art Nouveau to the demand for sumptuous hair ornaments for evening wear. A similar design, worn with feathers, illustrated in *Femina* (1912) was applauded for being well suited to the more natural looking, simplified hair styles that were replacing the high, padded pompadour coiffure.

PETIT PALAIS, MUSÉE DES BEAUX-ARTS DE LA VILLE DE PARIS

The outstretched wings, engraved with a feather pattern, and enameled translucent blue, enclose a large cushion-shaped citrine representing the sun. This motif, often combined with cobras, decorated the walls and doors of ancient Egyptian architecture and was revived by nineteenth-century designers for the decorative arts. Christopher Dresser, in his *Principles of Decorative Design* (1873), was so impressed by the severity, rigidity of line, and dignity of Egyptian ornament that he stated that he knew "of few instances where forms of an ornamental character have been combined in a manner either more quaint or more interesting than the example of the Winged disc or globe," which he identified as a symbol of protection. Since the Kensington firm of Child and Child (1880–1915) was patronized by William Holman Hunt and Sir Edward Burne Jones with others of the pre-Raphaelite circle, this tiara represents their taste.

TADEMA GALLERY, LONDON

The narrow band at the base of enameled laurel, centered on a citrine, is surmounted by a graduated sequence of five pointed arches with enameled details, each enclosing a fruit tree with gold leaves and sapphire and diamond berries. Supporting the arches are columns enameled with ivy leaves. Henry Wilson (1864–1934), an architect, set up his own workshop for making jewelry in 1895, and from 1901 taught in the metalwork department of the Royal College of Art. In the opinion of Janet Ashbee, married to another leading light of the Arts and Crafts movement, C. R. Ashbee, "Wilson looks like a seedy bank clerk yet is perhaps the greatest artist of the lot." He made several tiaras, the best known of which represents the legend of Orpheus and is in the collection of Goldsmith's Hall in London. This design, with its medieval echoes and naturalism, is typical of Wilson's approach, explained in his textbook, *Silverwork and Jewelery* (1912): "Remember always to have a bit of the natural foliage near you as a guide … never do anything in the way of ornament without reference to nature."

THE SATALOFF AND CLUCHEY FAMILY

The open-work band pinned with pearls is surmounted by plant motifs centered on a pair of dolphins to each side of a tall plant. James Cromar Watt (1862–1940) was an architect, collector of oriental art, and follower and friend of Henry Wilson. Having mastered the techniques of enameling and stone setting, he opened a gallery in Aberdeen, where he held exhibitions at regular intervals. The aquatic theme is not only expressed by the fish, the plants, and the sea green color of the enamel, but also by the pearls, fished from the rivers of his native Scotland.

THE SATALOFF AND CLUCHEY FAMILY

The tiara is formed by a sequence of dragonflies with sapphire eyes set wing-to-wing along the base and top, with moonstones filling the space between and above. Designed to wear over a modern bridal veil, the dragonflies are inspired by those in the Tiffany Archive sketchbooks, dating from the turn of the century, and by the hat pin mounted with opals and demantoid garnets in platinum shown at the St. Louis Fair in 1904 (cf. P. Schneirla and P. Proddow, *Tiffany: 150 Years of Gems and Jewelry,* 1987, plate 16.) It pays homage to the memory of Louis Comfort Tiffany, who was in charge of the company's Artistic Jewelry Department from 1907 to 1918.

TIFFANY & CO.

The tiara, convertible into a necklace, consists of five sections, each of gold wire wrought into a network of cells filled with a rich pattern of royal blue and emerald green *plique à jour* enamel, enlivened with flashes of ruby red. The bright blues echo the color of the cushion-shaped sapphire mounted in a collet to one side. It is a new version of a tiara/necklace created for Viscountess X in 1993, which has been seen at state openings of Parliament and other London events ever since. Marit Aschan, who held her first exhibition in 1948, has won an international reputation for her enamels, particularly for her mastery of the exacting "window" or *plique à jour* technique used here. She not only has the ideas, but brings them to fulfillment with her own hands in her own kiln, which accounts for the remarkable individuality of this piece of jewelry, made for the current exhibition.

MARIT GUINNESS ASCHAN

↑ DRAGONFLY TIARA   1998   TIFFANY & CO., AMERICAN
White gold, sapphires, moonstones.

↓ MILLENNIUM TIARA   1999   MARIT GUINNESS ASCHAN, ENGLISH
Gold, enamel, sapphire.

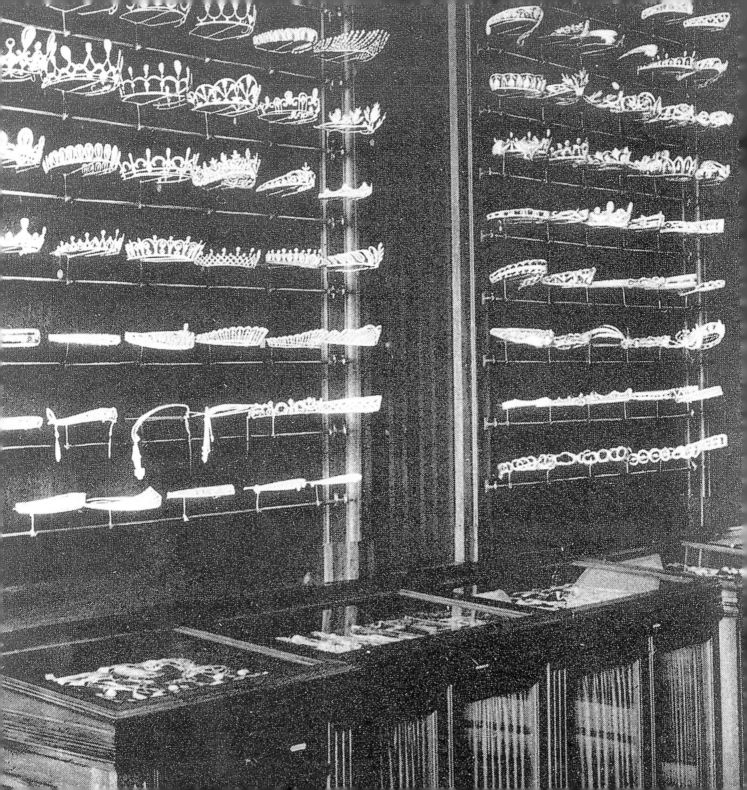

Chaumet possesses a unique collection of nickel silver replicas of every tiara made by the firm since the turn of the century. Formerly displayed on the walls of a room created for them, the Salle des Modèles, these vestiges of past glories never failed to impress the young brides who tried on the various designs to discover which one was the most flattering.

The diversity of the designs is astonishing. There are the romantic princely and ducal crowns created for princesses and duchesses and the highly political fleurs-de-lis favored by supporters of the Bourbons in exile. Best suited for the display of important stones were the arcaded tiaras either surmounted by pear-shaped pearls, cabochon rubies, or emeralds, or hung with briolette diamonds that swung with every movement of the head. The naturalistic motifs—pinks, ferns, ivy, holly, bull rushes, and daisies—were usually executed in small stones impeccably mounted into a glittering mosaic.

From the eighteenth century derived the popular ribbon motif tied into knots, combined with swags and tassels and the rococo network or trellis. As for the neoclassical themes—laurel, olive, ears of corn, palmettes, acanthus, volutes—the Greek-key pattern (both angular and curved) seems to have been the favorite here.

The many versions of the halo-shaped "Russian tiara" were made not only for the Grand Duchess Vladimir and Countess Torby but for the English duchess of Westminster, the French Mrs. Hope Vere, and for Baroness Lambert. The V-shaped Mary Stuart design was often combined with trails of leaves or feathers. Inspired by the heavens, the series of stars, crescent moons, and triple suns were ideally suited to display diamonds under blazing electric light. It is clear from the size of the collection that the demand for tiaras did not end with the Belle Epoque but continued strong in the interwar years. What changed was the style. In accordance with the principles of Art Deco, simplification became the rule, and abstract geometric motifs—lozenges, circles, and ovals—entered the vocabulary of design.

Photograph (undated) of the nickel
silver replicas installed in Chaumet's
Salle des Modèles.

CHAUMET ARCHIVES

This book is a companion to the exhibition Crowning Glories: Two Centuries of Tiaras, presented by the Museum of Fine Arts, Boston. The following is a complete checklist of the tiaras and other works of art in the order they appear in the exhibition. Works appearing only in the book are credited in the lists of additional picture credits and additional credits for artwork that follow the checklist.

Portrait of Empress Marie Louise, 1812
Robert Lefèvre (French, 1775–1830)
Oil on canvas
Collection Chaumet, Paris
[page 59]

Replica of the ruby & diamond parure of Empress Marie Louise, c. 1900
Joseph Chaumet (French, 1852–1928)
Gold, garnets, white sapphires.
Collection Chaumet, Paris
[page 58]

Bandeau, c. 1810
Nitot & Fils (?), Paris
Gold, pearls, nicolo intaglios.
Mikimoto
[page 57]

Festoon tiara, c. 1830
German
Gold, silver, button and pear
  pearls, diamonds.
S.J. Phillips Ltd., London
[page 65]

Topaz parure, 1820s
English (?)
Gold, golden topazes.
Private Collection
[page 67]

Fitzwilliam tiara, c. 1820
English
Gold, silver, diamonds.
The Trustees of the Rt. Hon. Olive, Countess
  Fitzwilliam's Chattels Settlement, By
  Permission of Lady Juliet Tadgell
[page 71]

Heathcote tiara, c. 1800 and later
English
Gold, silver, diamonds.
Baroness Willoughby de Eresby
[page 69]

Primrose Tiara, c. 1830 and later
English
Gold, silver, diamonds.
The Earl and Countess of Rosebery
[page 71]

Summer tiara, c. 1835
English
Gold, carnelians, amethysts, garnets,
  aquamarines, peridots, chrysoprases,
  citrines, turquoises, pearls.
Museum of London
[page 73]

Tiara and brooch, c. 1840
Neapolitan
Coral, gilt metal.
Museum of London
[page 75]

Queen Hortense's coronet, c. 1810
French
Jet, gilt bronze.
Musée National de Malmaison
[page 61]

Mourning parure, c. 1810
German
Iron, gold.
Albion Art, Japan
[page 63]

The Empress Eugénie's tiara, 1853
Gabriel Lemonnier (French, c. 1808–1884)
Gold, silver, pearls, diamonds.
Musée du Louvre, Département des Objets
  d'Art
[page 77]

Londonderry tiara, 1854
R.S. Garrard & Co., London
Gold, silver, diamonds.
The Londonderry Family
[page 79]

Queen Margherita's laurel tiara, 1867
Mellerio dits Meller, Paris
Gold, silver, diamonds.
Albion Art, Japan
[page 87]

Queen Margherita's "fender," c. 1870
Italian
Gold, silver, pearls, diamonds.
  Private Collection

Rosebery tiara, 1878
French (?)
Gold, silver, diamonds.
The Earl and Countess of Rosebery
[page 89]

Derby tiara, c. 1890
Skinner & Co.(?), London
Gold, silver, diamonds.
The Right Hon. the Earl of Derby
[page 89]

Scrollwork tiara, c. 1880
English
Gold, silver, diamonds, pear-shaped
 pearls.
Private Collection
[page 80]

Star tiara, c. 1870, remounted 1937
English
Gold, silver, diamonds, button pearls.
Private Collection
[page 91]

Pansy tiara, c. 1860
French (?)
Gold, silver, diamonds.
The Hon. Mrs. John Hastings Bass
[page 81]

Floral tiara, c. 1860
Mellerio dits Meller, Paris
Gold, silver, turquoises, diamonds.
Mellerio dits Meller Collection
[page 82]

Wild rose tiara, c. 1880
English
Gold, silver, diamonds.
Collection of John Yorke
[page 95]

The Willoughby Owl, 1860s
English
Gold, silver, diamonds, rubies, sapphires.
Private Collection
[page 93]

Gordon ivy tiara, 1869
R.G. Hennell (English)
Gold, silver, diamonds.
Private Collection
[page 93]

Oak leaf tiara, c. 1880
R.S. Garrard & Co., London
Gold, silver, pearls, diamonds.
Private Collection, U.K.
[page 95]

Buccleuch tiara, c. 1850
R.S. Garrard & Co., London
Gold, silver, turquoises, diamonds.
The Duke of Buccleuch, KT
[page 97]

Devonshire tiara, 1856
C.F. Hancock (English)
Gold, enamel, diamonds, cameos, intaglios.
The Duke of Devonshire and the Chatsworth
 Settlement Trustees
[page 99]

Archaeological Revival tiara, 1860s
Castellani, Rome
Gold, enamel, agate, glass beads.
The Sataloff and Cluchey Family
[page 101]

Peace tiara, 1860s
Mosaics Roman, setting English (?)
Gold, glass, mosaics.
Albion Art, Japan
[page 101]

The Grand Duchess Vladimir's tiara,
 c. 1870
Russian
Gold, silver, diamonds.
Private Collection
[page 103]

The Queen of Serbia's tiara, 1800s
Bolin (Russian)
Gold, silver, diamonds, paste replacement
 for emeralds.
Van Cleef & Arpels, Paris
[page 105]

Howe tiara, 1883
English
Gold, silver, diamonds.
Private Collection
[page 107]

Russian-style garland tiara, c. 1910
Fabergé, workmaster Fedor Afanassiev
 (Russian)
Platinum, enamel, diamonds.
Albion Art, Japan
[page 109]

Triple-sun tiara, c. 1910
French
Platinum, brilliants, gray pearl.
Private Collection
[page 111]

Mesh-pattern halo, c. 1910
Russian
Platinum millegrain, diamonds.
Thomas Färber
[page 111]

"Russian" tiara, 1908
Cartier, Paris
Platinum millegrain, diamonds, pearls.
Cartier Collection
[page 113]

Marghiloman tiara, 1914
Cartier, Paris
Steel, platinum, rubies, diamonds.
Cartier Collection
[page 115]

The Harcourt tiara, c. 1900
English (?)
Gold, silver, emeralds, diamonds.
Private Collection
[page 117]

The Iveagh tiara, c. 1900
R.S. Garrard & Co., London
Gold, silver, diamonds.
Private Collection
[page 118]

Talhouet tiara, c. 1908
Joseph Chaumet (French, 1852–1928)
Gold, silver, diamonds.
Collection Chaumet, Paris
[page 119]

Mountbatten tiara, c. 1910
French
Platinum millegrain, diamonds.
The Lady Pamela Hicks
[page 125]

Queen of the Belgians tiara, 1910
Cartier, Paris
Platinum millegrain, diamonds.
Cartier Collection
[page 127]

Bowknot tiara, c. 1900
Joseph Chaumet (French, 1852–1928)
Gold, silver, pink topazes, diamonds.
Collection Chaumet, Paris
[page 120]

Leafy-spray tiara, c. 1905
English
Platinum, diamonds, pearls.
Private Collection
[page 121]

Grand Duchess Hilda's tiara, 1907
Schmidt-Staub of Pforzheim (German)
Platinum, gold, diamonds.
Badisches Landesmuseum, Karlsruhe
[page 129]

Pendant drop tiara, c. 1910
Cartier, Paris
Platinum millegrain, diamonds.
Albion Art, Japan
[page 130]

Garland-style tiara, 1909
Cartier, Paris
Platinum millegrain, diamonds.
Private Collection
[page 131]

Laurel tiara, c. 1900
English
Gold, silver, diamonds.
Albion Art, Japan
[page 132]

Wheat-ear tiara, c. 1910
French (?)
Platinum millegrain, diamonds.
Private Collection
[page 133]

Key pattern tiara, 1913
Joseph Chaumet (French, 1852–1928)
Platinum millegrain, diamonds.
Private Collection
[page 137]

Labriffe bandeau, 1914
Joseph Chaumet (French, 1852–1928)
Platinum, diamonds.
Comtes de La Bretesche, Paris
[page 137]

Double bandeau, c. 1912
Boucheron, Paris
Platinum millegrain, diamonds.
Albion Art, Japan
[page 139]

Valkyrie wing tiara, 1907
Joseph Chaumet (French, 1852–1928)
Platinum, diamonds, translucent
   blue enamel.
Thomas Färber
[page 139]

Bourbon Parme tiara, 1919
Joseph Chaumet (French, 1852–1928)
Platinum millegrain, diamonds.
Thomas Färber
[page 142]

Preparatory sketch for advertisement, c. 1920
Anonymous, for Chaumet, Paris
Charcoal, goache, Chinese ink on tracing
   paper.
Collection Chaumet, Paris
[page 144]

Mauresque bandeau, 1922
Cartier, Paris
Platinum, coral, onyx, diamonds.
Cartier Collection

Persian bandeau, 1923
Cartier, Paris
Platinum millegrain, diamonds.
Cartier Collection
[page 141]

Divergent scroll tiara, c. 1930
Bulgari, Rome
Platinum, diamonds.
Albion Art, Japan
[page 143]

Bessborough tiara, 1931
Joseph Chaumet (French, 1852–1928)
Platinum, diamonds.
Mary, Countess of Bessborough
[page 149]

Egyptian style tiara, 1934
Cartier, London
Platinum, diamonds.
Cartier Collection
[page 151]

Topaz bandeau, 1937
Cartier, London
Platinum, gold, dark and light topazes.
Cartier Collection
[page 145]

Aquamarine tiara, 1937
Cartier, London
Platinum, aquamarines, diamonds.
Cartier Collection
[page 153]

Floral tiara, mid 1800s ·
English
Gold, silver, diamonds.
Smithsonian Institution, Washington, DC
[page 155]

Kemp tiara, 1894
Tiffany & Co., New York
Gold, platinum, diamonds.
Private Collection
[page 156]

Essex tiara, 1902
Cartier, Paris
Silver, gold, diamonds.
Cartier Collection
[page 159]

Oak leaf bandeau, 1920
Joseph Chaumet (French, 1852–1928)
Platinum, diamonds.
Private Collection
[page 158]

Doris Duke bandeau, c. 1930
Cartier
Platinum, diamonds, pearl.
Doris Duke Charitable Foundation
[page 165]

Brand tiara, 1935
Cartier, London
Platinum, turquoises, diamonds.
Cartier Collection
[page 157]

Whitney tiara, 1957
Fulco di Verdura (Italian, worked France
  and America, 1898–1978)
Gold, diamonds.
Collection Verdura, New York
[page 167]

Princess Grace tiara, 1976
French
Platinum, diamonds.
Van Cleef & Arpels, Paris
[page 169]

Autumn tiara, c. 1900
René Lalique (French, 1860–1945)
Gold, horn, diamonds, tortoiseshell.
Virginia Museum of Fine Arts, Richmond
[page 173]

Foliate bandeau, 1910
Georges Fouquet (French, 1862–1957)
Gold, silver, enamel, diamonds,
  aquamarines.
Petit Palais, Musée des Beaux-Arts de la
  Ville de Paris
[page 174]

Winged globe tiara, c. 1900
Child and Child (English, 1880–1915)
Silver, enamel, citrine.
Tadema Gallery, London
[page 175]

Gothic tiara, c. 1910
Henry Wilson (English, 1864–1934)
Gold, enamel, diamonds, sapphires, citrine.
The Sataloff and Cluchey Family
[page 176]

Dolphin tiara, c. 1900
James Cromar Watt (Scottish, 1862–1940)
Silver, enamel, freshwater pearls.
The Sataloff and Cluchey Family
[page 177]

Dragonfly tiara, 1998
Tiffany & Co., New York
White gold, sapphires, moonstones.
Tiffany & Co.
[page 181]

Millennium tiara, 1999
Marit Guinness Aschan (English, b. 1919)
Gold, enamel, sapphire.
Marit Guinness Aschan
[page 181]

Tiara Design Collection, c. 1900–1950
Chaumet, Paris
Nickel silver.
Collection Chaumet, Paris
[page 182]

PHOTO CREDITS

ACKNOWLEDGMENTS

Since owners of historic and beautiful jewelry are almost always reluctant to lend it, I must first express my deepest gratitude to all the private individuals who have made this exhibition possible. Similarly, I wish to thank the curators of museums who have also been kind enough to part with their treasures: Mr. Daniel Alcouffe of the Louvre; Madame Marie Christine Boucher, Mr. Gilles Chazal, and Mr. Dominique Morel of the Petit Palais; Mr. Bernard Chevallier of Malmaison; Dr. Reinhold Sanger of the Badisches Landesmuseum, Karlsruhe; Dr. Simon Thurley of the Museum of London; Dr. Jeffery E. Post of the Smithsonian Institution; and Dr. Katherine C. Lee of the Virginia Museum of Fine Arts. Very special thanks are due to Mr. Eric Nussbaum, who agreed to let us have all we requested from the Cartier collection, as did Mr. Kazumi Arikawa of Albion Art and Thomas Färber of Geneva. Other jewelers who have been generous are Mr. Eric Arpels of Van Cleef & Arpels; Mr. Kobayashi of Mikimoto; Mr. Olivier Mellerio; Mr. Ward Landrigan of Verdura; and Mrs. Sonia Newell Smith of Tadema Gallery, London. Those who have helped obtain objects and photographs are Ms. Anne Choate; Mr. Nicolas Luchsinger and Ms. Helen Teicher of Christie's; Ms. Daniele Turian and Ms. Lydia Creswell Jones of Sotheby's; Madame Marie Beauchard Moatti and Ms. Muffie Potter Aston of Van Cleef & Arpels; Ms. Stéphanie Mellerio and Ms. Anne Lawrence Imbert of Mellerio; Ms. Penny Proddow of Ralph Esmerian, New York; the Hon. Harry Fane; Dr. Helmut Seling; Mr. Ryo Yamaguchi; Mr. David Thomas of Asprey Garrard; Mr. Cyrille Boulay of Souvenirs du Gotha; Mr. René Brus; Dr. Richard Edgcumbe of the Victoria and Albert Museum; Ms. Cheryl Smith of the Museum of London; Mr. Peter Day, keeper of the collections at Chatsworth; Ms. Amanda Askari, curator of the collections of the earl of Derby at Knowsley; Mr. Horton Fawkes of the Spencer Collection at Althorp; Ms. Susan Bloom of the Doris Duke Charitable Foundation; Mr. Paul Miller of the Preservation Society of Newport County; Ms. Kathleen Schrader of the Virginia Museum of Fine Arts; Mr. Alan Goodrich of the John F. Kennedy Library; Ms. Elaine Hart and Mr. Richard Pitkin of the *Illustrated London News*; Ms. Anne Odom and Ms. Nancy Harris of Hillwood; and Ms. Annamarie Sandecki and Ms. Louisa Bann at the Tiffany Archives.

I must also thank all who have given valuable advice and introductions: Lady Abdy, Mr. Gabriel Badea-Paun, Mr. Yvon Guillaume Boscher, Mrs. Robert Charles, Mr. John Cornforth, Countess Angelika Coronnini von Cronberg, Ms. Angela Delaforce, Mr. Emmanuel Ducamp, Mrs. Angela Fischer, Ms. Michele Heuzé, Mr. Nicolas Handras, Ms. Roselyne Hurel, Mr. Jason Herrick, the late Mr. Ed Powys Jones, Mr. Kenneth Jay Lane, Mr. Ian Lowe, Mr. H. D. Lyon, Mr. Rupert Lord, Ms. Isabelle Lucas, Count Roland Lepic, Madame Irene de Maghalaes, Mrs. Elise Misiorowski, Mr. Derek Ostergard, Mrs. Nicholas Davie-Thornhill, and the Hon. Georgina Stonor.

Special thanks are due to Christophe Vachaudez, who shared his extensive royal jewelry archive with us, and has most kindly written the catalogue entries for the loans he secured for exhibition: The Grand Duchess Vladimir's Tiara, The Queen of Serbia's Tiara, Grand Duchess Hilda's Tiara, and the Liechtenstein Tiara. In London, Mr. Martin Norton, and his sons, Nicolas and Jonathan, and nephew Francis, have supported us with their customary generosity while their staff, especially Max Michelson and Michael Bell, have seen to repairs, valuations, photography, postage, and insurance with exemplary efficiency. I am most grateful to them all. As I discovered tiaras when writing the history, *Chaumet:*

Master Jewellers Since 1780, it gives me much pleasure to thank my friends there: Madame Beatrice de Plinval, Keeper of the Chaumet Collection, and Mr. Pierre Haquet, President of Chaumet International, S.A. Chaumet, famous for tiaras for the past two hundred years, not only lent some of the most valuable items from the collection in place Vendôme, but most kindly sponsored the exhibition.

I would also like to thank Dr. Malcolm Rogers, Ann and Graham Gund Director, who invited me to organize the exhibition, and the team at the Museum of Fine Arts, Boston, who have done so much to bring it about: Katie Getchell and Jennifer Bose (Exhibitions), Cynthia Purvis and Dacey Sartor (Publications), Valerie McGregor (Design), Patricia Loiko (Registrar), and Elizabeth Ann Coleman (Textile and Costume Department). With Susan Ward (also of the Textile and Costume Department), who has shared every single problem with me and solved most of them, I have had the happiest of collaborations.

—DIANA SCARISBRICK